ADOPT
ADAPT
FLOURISH

**AN EASY GUIDE TO ENGAGING AND
INSPIRING EMPLOYEES TO ADAPT TO CHANGE**

MELANIE FROK

Published in 2015 in Australia.
www.adaptusconsulting.com.au
Copyright © Melanie Frok 2015

Text copyright © Melanie Frok 2015
Cover Design: Scarlett Rugers Design
Layout Design: Book Cover Café

Printed in Australia.

National Library of Australia Cataloguing-in-Publication entry (pbk)

Creator: Frok, Melanie, author.

Title: Adopt adapt flourish: an easy guide to engaging and inspiring employees to adapt to change / Melanie Frok; illustrations, Brenda Brown.

ISBN: 9780992516802 (pbk)
             9780992516819 (ebk, Kindle)
             9780992516826 (ebk, ePub)

Subjects: Personnel management.
             Organisational change.
             Organisational behaviour.
             Employees--Attitudes.

Other Creators/Contributors: Brown, Brenda, illustrator.

Dewey Number: 658.3

ACKNOWLEDGEMENTS

To my daughter Olivia, whose generosity of spirit, love and joyfulness inspires me to live my dreams of being both a good mother and a successful business owner.

To my mother and father, who provided unfailing encouragement and support during the writing of this book and who travel alongside me with unconditional love in this journey called life.

To Andrew Griffiths and the KPI community, who inspired, supported and encouraged me and opened my eyes to a world of possibility.

Finally, to you, the reader, for having the courage to step outside your comfort zone and learn to embrace change with zest. May your business go from strength to strength.

DEDICATION

This book is dedicated to hard working small business owners everywhere who have the foresight, leadership, and courage to build strong, flourishing businesses where employees are engaged, energised and thriving.

TABLE OF CONTENTS

INTRODUCTION

WHEN THE RATE OF CHANGE INSIDE AN ORGANIZATION BECOMES SLOWER THAN THE RATE OF CHANGE OUTSIDE, THE END IS IN SIGHT

JACK WELCH – FORMER CEO, GENERAL ELECTRIC

We live in a fast-paced, competitive world. The 21st century has altered our lives by offering us new choices and never-before-imagined products. Not that long ago, we had to wait on an often slow dial-up connection to get Internet access. Our televisions weren't flat, handwritten letters had not yet been replaced by email and texting, an apple was just a fruit, only birds could twitter, and phones could only make phone calls. Now our society is driven by powerful Internet-connected desktops, software solutions for every business need, widely available Wi-Fi, and limitless cloud storage. And it's still changing.

All. The. Time.

Mastering social media, staying connected 24/7, and becoming world famous with one YouTube video is the new reality. We now *need* things that didn't exist five or ten years ago. Imagine trying to live your life today without iTunes, or Google, or Facebook. *Could you?*

Innovation is necessary. No business can prosper without some type of technology to operate, communicate or connect with employees and customers. A few businesses are still clinging to the old ways but their days are likely to be numbered. Part of today's business acumen is the ability to evolve. What happens when you can't evolve with the times? Well ... just think Kodak, Nokia and Blockbuster. All these are companies that failed to innovate and adapt, and now they're obsolete.

The fact that humans create constant change through intelligence and ingenuity is an interesting phenomenon. Yet, countless people don't like change; they fear it, reject it, and go to great lengths to avoid it. *Why is that?*

Many theorists suggest that workplace change invokes a feeling of loss of control and uncertainty. As creatures of habit, we can't help ourselves. It's diabolical, really ... as humans, we constantly engineer change and yet we are inherently opposed to it.

Part of human nature dictates that when we've been doing something a particular way for a long time, it *feels* like a good way to do things. And the longer we've been doing it that way, the more comfortable *it* is. So when something changes, it feels like we have to give up something good for something *uncomfortable* and perhaps inferior. This is the reality of change.

The process of giving something up that feels *easy* in order to embrace something new can feel off-balanced and difficult – even *painful*.

So if workplace change is vital to a business being able to flourish, how do you avoid employees feeling ambivalent or negative? How do you motivate them to accept and adapt to change?

Employee engagement is a powerful approach in dealing with resistance while also encouraging employees to accept change. Workers need to feel respected, appreciated, validated and valuable to build *any* business into a thriving, high-performing machine. If your team doesn't care about your business, they won't be motivated to adapt as it grows, meaning that your business will not reach its full potential. How to engage and inspire employees to adapt to change is challenging to even the most capable of leaders. It's one of the hardest things about the current business landscape and, as such, is the focus of this book.

HOW TO USE THIS BOOK

Adopt Adapt Flourish has been written with the realities of small to medium businesses in mind. The following pages are filled with numerous ways to lead your business through a significant change with less stress, less resistance, and as a result, in less time. The advice and techniques provided in this practical workbook use employee engagement as a tool that will ensure that any change within your business will stick.

It introduces the *Adapt Method*.

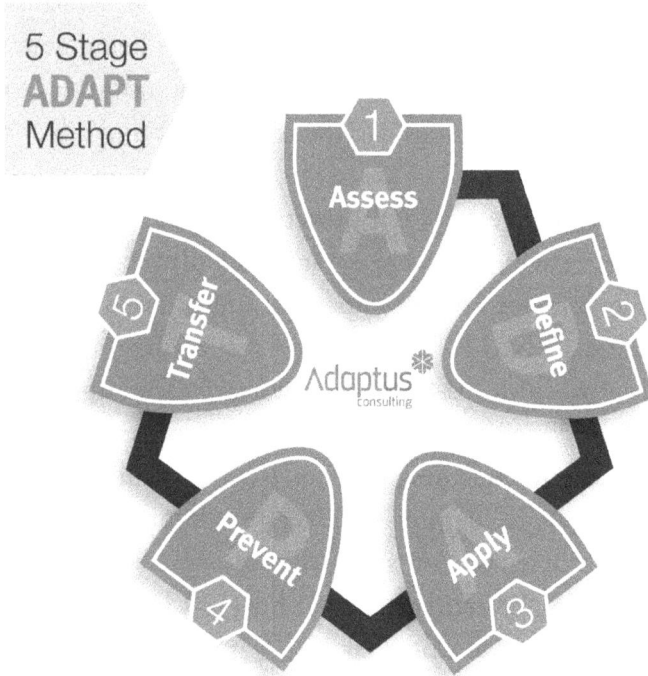

The concept comes from the scientific notion of *adaptation*. Consider your business like this: it's one-of-a-kind, so every new employee must adjust to the conditions of its unique environment once they are employed. They learn about the ways your business operates and then they perform (and in some cases, *adjust)* accordingly. Now imagine you change something – perhaps a new work procedure or operating model is introduced. Your business now needs people to *adapt* in order to accommodate the change. Every time you change something in your business, you are expecting your employees to modify their thinking and behaviour to suit a new or different purpose. The information within this book will help you do that.

The *Adapt Method* is an action-based approach that any motivated business owner can apply to lead their team into new territory. It will also help to get employees focused, enthused and performing in the direction the business needs to go – without the headache!

The five stages of the *Adapt Method* are:

1. **Assess**
   Assess how ready your business and employees are to make the change.

2. **Define**
   Define the activities needed to support your business and employees through the change.

3. **Apply**
   Apply the activities you have planned while your business is undergoing change.

4. **Prevent**
   Review what is and isn't working, and adjust the approach if required.

5. **Transfer**
   Transfer to the new way of working, lock it into your culture and sustain it so your business benefits from the investment in the change.

Adopt Adapt Flourish is full of easy exercises you can do yourself. Each exercise comes with instructions. Some include blank forms, referred to as templates, to assist you in carrying out the exercise. You don't need any special knowledge or skills, just a desire and determination to engage and support your employees through a change-over period.

A stage may run in parallel or overlay another stage. It is not always a linear process. You need to exercise judgement on your business needs, employee preferences, and your culture.

*For your convenience, the blank templates are also available for free download at **www.adaptusconsulting.com.au***

SUMMARY

The guidance and advice provided throughout this book is underpinned by the work of world leaders in business change and advancements in employee engagement philosophy. Implementing a change and dealing with defiance and opposition can be stressful and time consuming, both of which can cause your business to suffer. This book will help you focus your leadership time and effort on the right activities to ensure that resistance doesn't hurt your bottom line.

If you believe that people matter but you want to spend less time dealing with issues and more time getting on with making money, start helping your employees adapt well today.

CHAPTER 1

BEING CAPABLE OF MANAGING CHANGE WELL IS THE NEW COMPETITIVE EDGE

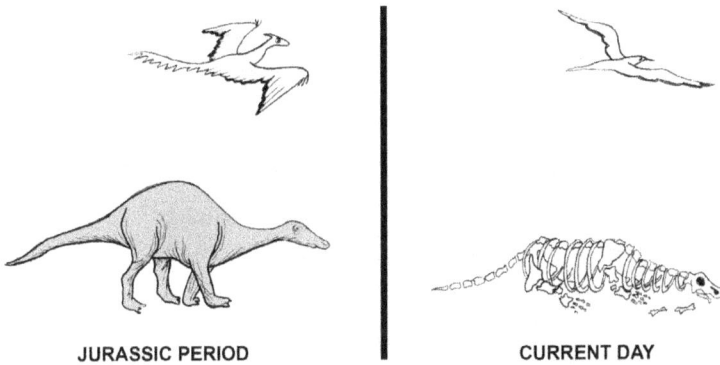

JURASSIC PERIOD | CURRENT DAY

IT IS NOT THE STRONGEST OF THE SPECIES THAT SURVIVES, NOR THE MOST INTELLIGENT. IT IS THE ONE THAT IS MOST ADAPTABLE TO CHANGE.

CHARLES DARWIN – SCIENTIST

Small and medium businesses represent 96% of all trading companies in Australia. However, the chance of any new business failing in the first five years is very high. According to the Australian Bureau of Statistics, one of the key barriers to business longevity is the lack of ability to implement innovative change. How a company made money five years ago, or even two years ago, may not position it for prosperity today. To survive your business needs to adapt to change.

Influences and pressure from globalisation, technological advances, economic reforms, regulatory modifications, climatic impacts, competition, innovation, acquisitions, outsourcing, expansion – the list goes on – will affect how a business must evolve. Some changes like new technology that offers efficiency and diversification, are welcomed. While others – like new players entering the market and making their presence felt – may cause fear and anxiety.

Consider these examples for a moment:

- Ten years ago job vacancies were simply advertised in the Saturday paper. Today, 94% of recruitment in Australia is generated using SEEK and LinkedIn. The creation of the global online skills marketplace has revolutionised the way people search for jobs and find candidates.
- The job title of Application Developer didn't exist before the iPhone was created back in 2007. The surge of demand for new applications has fostered a $15 billion revenue stream for Apple ever since.
- New careers in Social Media have sprouted as industry embraces online social networks to reach out to customers and communicate. And who could overlook the new Cloud Computing Consultant – every tech-savvy Millennial's dream job.
- Remember going into a bookstore? It's hard to even find a bricks and mortar bookshop these days. Now you buy a book online and it might be freighted from anywhere in the world to your door. Or it arrives instantly to your smart-device. In fact, nearly any product or service can be sourced and arranged for delivery online direct to your door today.

And let's not ignore what's coming. What change can we expect to impact our lives and become the next must-have? Depending on what you read or who you believe, it could be virtual or augmented reality or other more useful technologies like enterprise mobile applications that will drastically change the world of work in the decade to come.

HOW WELL YOUR BUSINESS ADAPTS TO CHANGE AND HOW FAST, WILL DETERMINE WHETHER YOU LEAD THE PACK OR FOLLOW IT

Worldwide, there is growing recognition that a business's *adaptability* – how flexible and responsive a business is – determines if it leads the competition or follows it. Focusing on productivity alone may work in the short term but if you want your business to become, or remain, a market-leader then you must focus on the state of your business's adaptability – how able your business is to respond to change faster than your competitors.

One of the greatest challenges for business owners is knowing whether their decisions are enabling growth or constraining it. Whether you're introducing new processes, new technology or a new function, you need your employees to be on board and motivated to act. Employees who are inspired and willing to improve the way your business does things create an adaptive culture and positions your business as a top performer.

It is easy to fall into the trap of viewing current-day success as proof that you have an engaged workforce. It's not until you understand that engagement is something that requires work to create and sustain that you realise that getting the best out of people is an art in itself.

Undoubtedly, you have employees who do not like change or who go out of their way to avoid it. That's not unusual. Uncertain, anxious and confused employees who feel out of control and don't know what to expect do not perform well. If you want to engage your workforce to embrace change but don't know how, applying the *Adapt Method* will substantially increase your chances for success.

WHY POORLY MANAGED CHANGE WILL FAIL TO DELIVER A RETURN

Responding to global market forces is becoming more complex. Businesses have to look beyond performance and find innovative ways to stand out. This reality puts pressure on business owners to introduce creative solutions to what's challenging or ailing their bottom line. Solving problems and planning for future events requires change. Yet many business-change efforts fail to live up to expectations, new ventures regularly fall short on delivering a financial return, and employees' performance often declines while the environment is adjusting. What goes wrong?

Typically, there are three reasons why business-change doesn't deliver on its promise:

1. Disengaged employees are slow to adapt to new ways of working and leaders usually lack the skill and know-how to motivate them.

2. Managing change is time-consuming and messy when you don't know how. Leaders rarely know how to step back

from the disorder so they can lead with clarity, leaving the change-effort struggling in a sea of turbulence.

3. If obstacles to the change process exist in the business model, the chance of the change being successful is limited. Often, leaders don't know how to recognise or remove them.

The end result is rather lackluster and predictable. The opportunity to grow the bottom line is lost because employees don't embrace the change or connect to where the business needs to go.

ACTIVELY ENGAGING EMPLOYEES HELPS TO DRIVE PROFIT

Unlike big corporations, whose wheels turn ever so slowly, smaller businesses can capitalise on their size and flex when fluctuations affect the economy and local markets. This agility, coupled with unleashing the enthusiasm and energy in a workforce, brings about innovation and creativity. A person's full potential is activated when they are engaged – using both their head, and their heart. Following the logic that well-motivated people just perform better, it stands to reason that improving the level of engagement with employees will boost your revenue growth.

High employee engagement has been correlated to high productivity and performance levels across all sectors of the economy globally. Adaptability is also linked to the factors that keep employees happy, challenged and engaged. Research supports the notion that if employees don't adopt change effectively, nothing much profitable happens. Making change stick is not an event, but a dynamic process that unfolds over time. Engagement is the bridge between just installing a change into your business and actually realising the benefit through employees' productivity, over time.

Has your business's past efforts to introduce change achieved the results you expected in the timeframe you wanted? Most business owners have never tried to *manage* change, they just let it happen. Or they don't feel capable of managing people through it effectively, so they just marshal it in and hope for the best. Hoping for the best, however, is not a strategy for success.

CASE STUDY: HOW NOT TO IMPROVE CUSTOMER SERVICE

A company introduced a new set of customer service principles to their business. The doctrine was very sound and even quite inspiring. It clearly framed the way they wanted employees to think about customers and treat them. Unfortunately, this new cultural ideology just landed on people's desks and inboxes one day out of the blue. Although many employees had no issue with the intent, few people had been engaged to *believe* in the strategy. This resulted in management's aspiration having very little impact on the day-to-day interaction between employees and customers.

Taking a *no-engagement* approach sets your business up for failure no matter how good a new idea is. Don't make this mistake; learn to engage your workforce. It will be more profitable in the end.

SUMMARY

No matter what your industry, to stay competitive your business must reshape and embrace change. Businesses that become good at adapting to change are more likely to be around for the long term. If your workforce can adapt to change faster than your opposition, then you have a strong, competitive advantage. There's never been a better time to learn how to flex and build change resilience in your business to ensure your long-term growth and prosperity.

THE MISTAKES BUSINESSES MAKE WHEN UNDERGOING CHANGE

I CANNOT SAY WHETHER THINGS WILL GET BETTER IF WE CHANGE, WHAT I CAN SAY IS THEY MUST CHANGE IF THEY ARE TO GET BETTER

GEORGE L. LICHTENBERG – SCIENTIST

Implementing something new can disrupt your business and harm productivity if not managed well. Feeling disappointed about the results of poorly managed change is common. The process of altering someone's behaviour disturbs their sense of control and pushes them out of their comfort zone – it makes them feel uncertain, sometimes even incompetent and this can lead to problems.

Does this sound familiar? *I'm happy doing what I'm doing. This is the way we've always done it around here. If it ain't broke don't fix it.* Often the problems that cause the disappointment come from common mistakes leaders make when they don't know how to manage change well. This chapter will reveal the Top 10 mistakes made when introducing change, and how to avoid them.

CASE STUDY: MANAGING CHANGE ALWAYS COMES WITH TEETHING PROBLEMS

John owns a large dental clinic. After attending an industry seminar, he decided to invest in a new customer relationship management technology. John envisaged cost-savings, more repeat business and happier employees.

Not long after the new system was installed John noticed problems. What he had failed to understand was that the mindsets of his employees were deeply entrenched in the old system and habitual ways of working. The benefits of the new system depended on John's team being motivated to use it in a new way – which they had not – and resistance was rife.

John lacked the know-how to resolve his team's resistance and was forced to revert his business back to using the old system. He lost his investment and it took months for his practice to recover from the disruption. John's mistakes were lack of engagement about where the business wanted to go, lack of communication about the benefits and lack of training in improved practices.

Don't be a John! Learn how to take active steps towards managing change in your workplace. Increase the odds significantly in your favour by taking conscious actions to create an engaged, motivated workforce during times of change.

THE TOP 10 MISTAKES REVEALED AND HOW TO AVOID THEM

Here we look at the most common mistakes business owners make when shaking up their product and service environment and how to avoid them.

Mistake	Explanation	How to avoid this mistake
1. No Change Goal is created to bring people together	A clear and compelling Change Goal has a powerful effect in bonding people together towards a common purpose – making the change happen. If the need for change is not understood, your employees won't become emotionally charged to make the right adjustments. Having a strong Change Goal for all to rally around that connects the business goal to the value for people often drives complacency away. Without urgency most people won't feel compelled to put in any extra effort to achieve change.	Refer to Chapter 5

25

Mistake	Explanation	How to avoid this mistake
2. The *What's in it for me?* is not clear	When employees don't understand the reasons why the business is changing, the risks involved if there is no change, or what the business is trying to achieve is not clear, they are much less likely to support the direction your business is trying to move to. Without knowing where the business is heading and what new opportunities will be created, there is less buy-in or belief in the outcome of the change. The biggest barrier to success when a business undergoes change is changing minds and attitudes. When employees don't understand what's in the change for them, or can't link the change to the value and the purpose of the new way to operate in their job, they will not champion the goal. Business leaders need to connect every employee to the importance of where they are taking the company and how it offers advantages to employees in equal measure.	Refer to Chapter 5
3. Change is not managed, it's just marshaled in	When minimal or no planning is done to create ways to lead and support employees through change, time gets wasted, workflow is disrupted, and chaos often ensues.	Refer to Chapters 6, 7, 8, 9, 10, 11

Mistake	Explanation	How to avoid this mistake
4. Training is used as the only connection between the old and the new work practices	Training often doesn't address the social skills and attitudes needed back on the job. It's not until employees are required to practise in their normal day-to-day working environment that true skills transfer can take effect. On-the-job practice to complement skill and knowledge training is vital to ensuring that a workplace change sticks.	Refer to Chapters 7, 12
5. Everything about the change is under-communicated	When the Change Goal, benefits and new opportunities for the organisation and employees are under-communicated or unclear, confusion becomes widespread. Extra time and effort is then required to reset people's understanding down the track.	Refer to Chapter 12

Mistake	Explanation	How to avoid this mistake
6. Actively engaging employees is not made an important part of the process	When employees are not given an opportunity to be involved during a transition, they can feel disempowered, fearful or out-of-control. Feeling held back or confused can stop employees from delivering to their full potential, or, worse, they stop trying. This is often the reason why productivity goes into decline during a transition. Active employee involvement will turn into enthusiasm, which will turn into action, which will help make the change a success.	Refer to Chapter 12
7. No feedback is sought or given and good ideas are not recognised	When a business doesn't ask its employees for feedback, mistakes are not detected and inefficiencies are not resolved. A continuous improvement culture can only be cultivated on the foundation of genuine feedback. And if you do collect feedback but don't recognise or reward employees who speak up, then the effort is seen as not valued and people stop bothering.	Refer to Chapter 13

Mistake	Explanation	How to avoid this mistake
8. Obstacles that stop people from embracing change are not cleared	Sometimes the blocks are in people's heads, other times in the organisation's operational structure; it can even come down to a particular individual who is acting as an obstruction to the change. Wherever the obstacles exist they must be identified and removed. Organisational barriers can make adapting to change insurmountable for employees.	Refer to Chapter 13
9. The effort to foster people's adoption of the change stops too soon	It's a big mistake to withdraw support too early. Until the change is deeply embedded into the business culture, the shift in thinking and behaving may still regress to the old ways of working. Behaviour change must be regularly checked to ensure people are not reverting back to former work practices. If they are, then extra support needs to be added to put them back on the right path again.	Refer to Chapter 14
10. Resistance is ignored or dealt with badly	People-driven resistance to change is often ignored, dealt with badly, or seen as too difficult when hard decisions need to be made to address it. The consequences are sometimes irreversible, sometimes catastrophic. Typically morale is damaged, belief in the value of the change is weakened, and the progress of change slows down.	Refer to Chapter 15

Research shows that employee resistance is the single biggest factor that results in business change failure. Identifying resistance and eliminating it may be the difference between being successful or wasting valuable time, money and resources dealing with problems that appear when people don't or won't adopt a change.

THE 10 MOST COMMON REASONS WHY EMPLOYEES RESIST CHANGE

Here are the most common reasons why resistance emerges during a change effort.

1. Employees lack an understanding of why the change is needed or the consequences to the business of not changing.

2. The business leader is not visible or doesn't participate or role model the changed behaviours.

3. Employees are not aware of the benefits the change will bring to their work life, they don't know – *what's in it for me?*

4. A perception or fear exists that the change will have a negative impact on workload or responsibilities, or cause job losses.

5. Employees lack clarity about their role after it has been impacted by the change.

6. Employees are comfortable, or entrenched in the old ways of working – they don't want to change.

7. Scepticism exists that people are willing to change, or the change will deliver the benefits, or the business can even deliver the change – employees don't *believe it.*

8. The immediate supervisor is negative about the change or creates barriers to others trying to make the change.

9. Poor, insufficient or irrelevant communication exists across the business, or is given at the wrong time, or to the wrong audience.

10. The culture is complacent, conservative and indifferent and change is counter-cultural – typically sentiments are *We've never needed to change before, so why now?*

CASE STUDY: EMPLOYEE RESISTANCE CAN COME OUT OF THE BLUE

A financial broker introduced a new assessment tool to calculate mortgage lending suitability for new customers. During training and in the weeks leading up to the change-over, employees were observed as competently able to use the new tool. However, when the old tool was switched off, performance data was showing that fewer loans were being assessed using the new tool compared with before. Resistance had set in. But why?

It was discovered that employees felt the new risk assessment tool unfairly scrutinised low-income earners. Unbeknownst to management, employees had created a workaround and they were using it to avoid using the new tool. This caused management a lot of time and effort to identify a strategy to resolve the issue and get employees on board using the new assessment tool.

Further communication was required to explain that, in fact, unfair bias against low-income earners was not the case, but different criteria had to be used so the financier could comply with APRA, the Australian financial services governing body. This meant that in some instances a different outcome was inevitable but that it was in the best interests of both the customer and the money lender not to proceed with the loan. When employees understood the rationale they more willingly complied with the new process.

COMMUNICATION AND EMPATHY – THE KEYS TO DEALING WITH RESISTANCE

At its core, managing people through change is primarily a talkfest. Open, transparent, authentic communication is the single most effective way to avoid resistance. The key to handling resistance when it does occur is to use empathy in your communication.

Empathy is the ability to be mindful of the feelings, thoughts or attitudes of another. Being sensitive to another person's feelings makes it possible to have an effect on their ability to change.

Empathy is a difficult, somewhat foreign concept in a business environment, but a necessary one if you want a positive outcome.

Don't come at resistant behaviour as though you want to argue or defend or fight. It's not about winning or losing, it's about understanding what the problem is, and trying to work together to find a solution. Exercising empathy will help you deal with an employee's doubts about the change and build their will to adopt the new behaviours.

BE PREPARED TO LISTEN AND ACT

Resistance can be quickly and easily identified and addressed when you are open to feedback and, possibly, criticism. Dealing effectively with resistance boils down to your appetite to understand the issues and find solutions. Some of the time that will mean allowing your employees to come up with the solution and sometimes it will be about you changing your own leadership style, behaviour or investing time or money into creating a more attractive and acceptable environment. At its most extreme it may mean letting an employee go and hiring someone more like-minded. Whatever it takes, you can manage resistance and achieve a favourable outcome for both your business and your employees if you are willing to listen and act.

HOW TO IDENTIFY MORE SUBTLE INDICATORS OF RESISTANT BEHAVIOUR

Most examples of resistant behaviour will show themselves quite openly, but some resistance is harder to detect. If you are savvy enough to want to get on top of resistance before it surfaces, here are some tactics you can use to proactively uncover it.

Using this approach ...	You can discover ...
• Casual discussion • Via the grapevine • Attendance records • Observing body language and non-verbal cues when the change is discussed	Changes in behaviour that indicate a person is not on board. Examples include: • absenteeism • not providing information on request • using workarounds when the new behaviour should be being used • being disinterested in the change • reluctant to take ownership of change activities • passive resistance – a person verbally supports the change but is unwilling to comply with the new rules of operation
• Meetings • Interviews • Focus groups • Email • Social media • Change-ready assessments • Feedback tools • Surveys	Changes in communication that can indicate resistance. Examples include: • not being forthcoming with feedback when asked • lack of interest in group discussions about the change • complaining or asking negative, loaded, or redundant questions in meetings, interviews or training sessions

Using this approach ...	You can discover ...
Seek anecdotal feedback from leaders and supervisors who are in a position to observe resistant behaviour	The existence of widespread resistant behaviour. Examples include: • old systems being used instead of new ones • observations of disengagement or anxious behaviour • lack of belief in the benefits of the change • lack of co-operation or bad mouthing the business's attempts to change

WHATEVER YOU DO, DON'T DO THIS!

There's no doubt that managing resistance is tough. But don't make it harder on yourself by making these mistakes:

• Don't neglect dealing with resistance – it won't go away on its own, and over time it is likely to get worse.

• Don't assume you know the reason for the resistance. It's not until you listen to what the resistor has to say that you can get to the bottom of the issue.

• Don't use a *just do it* approach – it won't work, and it will just make it harder for you to achieve your goals.

• Don't shut down communication to resistors – that only fans the fire.

• Don't confront resistors in public – always address the behaviour in private.

• Never use fear or threats – this only encourages supporters of the change to reconsider their position once they know a colleague is in peril.

BELIEVE IT OR NOT, RESISTANCE HAS ITS ADVANTAGES

Resistance is a good sign that something is happening, that change is being felt. It's hard to fathom, but there are advantages to feeling resistance from your workforce against the effort to change. Resistance highlights that something in your change effort needs altering or improving – it's a source of feedback. It is also a sign that your engagement effort has fallen short. Resistance is a red flag that you've dropped the ball somewhere, and you need to identify the problems and fix them.

SUMMARY

These typical mistakes can slow down the progress of change, create unnecessary resistance, or permanently damage the productivity level you had before you got started. Luckily, they are avoidable. By following the *Adapt Method* you can wipe out the common problems you may encounter when your business is growing and evolving.

In the next chapter, we will look at the importance of employee engagement and how a motivated workforce contributes to introducing business change successfully.

CHAPTER 3

EMPLOYEE ENGAGEMENT IS IMPORTANT TO YOUR BOTTOM LINE

RALPH! I EXPECT YOU TO COME TO WORK NEAT AND WELL-GROOMED!

IF YOU DON'T HAVE SELF-AWARENESS, IF YOU CAN'T HAVE EMPATHY, THEN NO MATTER HOW SMART YOU ARE, YOU ARE NOT GOING TO GET VERY FAR

DANIEL GOLEMAN – AUTHOR

Organisations' that get engagement right consistently outperform their competitors. How employees *feel* while spending time at work has an impact on commercial success. Engaged teams are significantly more productive, have less employee turnover, absenteeism, and fewer safety incidents.

Unleashing enthusiasm in a workforce brings about higher productivity. Often businesses undergoing change experience it as both challenging and rewarding. For employees it can feel disruptive and disempowering. Businesses who show employees they are genuinely valued, and who create a buzz of energy in the workplace, especially when in transition, perform better in today's economy.

Unlike volatile market forces, the level of employee engagement in your business is within your control. To win customers – and a bigger share of the marketplace – companies must first win the hearts and minds of their employees. When it comes to managing change, instead of *telling* people what to do, they need to be inspired to do it.

IGNORE ENGAGEMENT – AT WHAT COST?

The consequences to your bottom line of ignoring engagement can be substantial. If your people are disengaged and you are trying to implement something new or make a change, then you run the risk of one or more of these issues derailing your change efforts:

- Your change will not deliver all of the financial value that you expected to receive.
- Your productivity levels will fall because your workforce will only partially adapt, or will be slow to adapt to the change.
- Your business focus will shift to dealing with resistance issues.
- The opportunity for you to grow your market share will diminish or be lost.

Building strong engagement between people takes time and focused action. Each person has their own unique perception of the world, their own ideas, feelings and mindsets. Suggesting your employees *just do it*, and ignoring their individuality puts you on a fast track to failure.

OUT WITH THE OLD AND IN WITH THE NEW

Australian workers today expect a lot more from their jobs, their bosses and their working environments. The traditional Australian way – salary, superannuation and a 38-hour work week – is no longer enough. Talented employees are not afraid to leave an employer and go to another to get their expectations and personal, intrinsic needs met. Like it or not, a growing assumption of employees today is that working is not just about the basics of paid performance, training and promotions. In the current competitive markets, work has become a place to nurture enthusiasm, passion, strengths and an individual's edge.

Over the past two decades, one of the most impactful changes in the world of work has been in the approach to directing employees. The old industrialised regime 'managed' workers in the past by planning, organising and controlling everything. This is unfeasible today. Truly great businesses create an environment where each individual is valued and they can contribute meaningfully. Businesses that win in their industry and in the modern world have an ignited workforce that is clear on purpose, connected, and feeling fully alive in what they do and how they do it.

WHAT DOES IT MEAN FOR EMPLOYEES TO BE ENGAGED?

Employee engagement does not just mean people are happy or satisfied. A person can appear happy but that doesn't automatically mean they are working productively or care about your business. Equally, a person that appears to be satisfied does not mean they are committed to your business and its goals.

Engagement describes feelings, thoughts, and behaviour. It is a voluntary reaction and an attitude an employee has towards fully contributing to the health of your business.

To summarise engagement, it means that a person is feeling or demonstrating several of the following characteristics:

- They are emotionally invested in, excited about and committed to their work over-and-above their standard duties.
- They are willing to become involved in, or be enthusiastic about, work activities.
- They are focused on the task at hand, and not easily distracted.
- There is a willingness to positively contribute to growth and revenue opportunities.
- They are actively promoting the business's products and services.
- They consistently encourage their co-workers to perform better.
- They are willing to create value for the business, every day.

Employee engagement is an emotional – heart and mind – commitment your employees have to the success of your business and its goals.

THE DISCRETIONARY EFFORT RIFT

Employees who care for the role they perform and the business they work in don't work just for the money or what they can get out of the arrangement. They willingly give of themselves to contribute and fulfill business goals because they value what they do and the nature of the business. When employees nurture and protect your business – when they are *engaged* – they are using their discretionary effort. Discretionary effort is the energy, positive attitude and labour employees give to their job, over-and-above the minimum required.

What makes discretionary effort so valuable to a business is it's voluntary for the employee to give it.

If you manage a team or run a company, you likely hire people with the expectation that they'll put in their best effort, every day, to help your business succeed. Unfortunately, this is Utopia. Over time many employees slip into performing just enough to get by, enough to not get fired. For example, they may stop generating improvement ideas, they may perform more slowly, make mistakes, generate poor quality, or reluctantly drag themselves to work, unmotivated and disengaged. A gap between best efforts and just doing OK develops. In engagement terms, this gap forms the *discretionary effort rift* – the difference between someone doing his or her best everyday and performing just well enough to get by.

Emotions play a far greater role in determining business outcomes than many leaders grasp. Despite sound research recommending that businesses create engaged teams, the Australian work culture is not getting better at creating meaningful work situations, and disengagement is commonplace. For example, apathy and absenteeism result in missed opportunities, reduced productivity, and increased stress on the employees left to pick up the slack.

According to corporate research giant Gallup, a staggering 76% of all Australian workers are disengaged and detached from their jobs, preferring to be somewhere else, doing something else. According to this research it costs Australia $55 billion per year in lost productivity. Just think about the statistics for a moment. For every one hundred people you employ, potentially up to seventy-six of them lack focus, or feel little to no emotional investment in your business. This means that your environment is much less productive than it could be. How much time and money is your business wasting?

EMPATHY – THE JEWEL IN YOUR LEADERSHIP CROWN

Empathy is a vital skill in enabling engagement and successfully changing the way your workforce operates. What does it mean to show empathy? Empathy can be described as understanding the feelings, thoughts and attitudes of others – in other words, the ability to *put yourself in the shoes of another person*. It can be learned, so if you've never considered it with regards to your employees, don't despair. Communication, sharing, authenticity and trust are the key

CHAPTER 3

behaviours that demonstrate empathy. For example, learning to do something new usually involves a temporary decline in performance levels. Typically, a person becomes very focused on getting the new thing right, which adds time to the process. Acknowledging this factor and allowing for it shows empathy.

WHY EMPATHY IS IMPORTANT IN BUSINESS

Human beings are emotional at their core; practicing empathy will help you to manage people's responses to the business change you're bringing in. Empathy is the underpinning value of the *Adapt Method*. All of the techniques used in the *Adapt Method* encourage you to identify with the feelings, thoughts, attitudes and experiences of your employees ... not in an insincere way but genuinely, to enable connection, and to engage the hearts and minds of the people your business is so reliant on for success.

ENGAGED WORKFORCES OUTPERFORM THEIR COMPETITORS

Businesses with high employee engagement outperform their competitors, even in periods of economic downturn.

High employee engagement has been proven to:
- increase shareholder return, annual net income, productivity, performance and profit margins
- increase the generation of innovation and ideas
- improve customer service, customer loyalty and repeat business

43

- increase employee advocacy and loyalty
- reduce costs associated with absenteeism, production errors, accidents and inefficient processes
- reduce employee turnover (replacement can cost anywhere up to 150% of the departing employee's salary).

Although some business owners might expect employees to separate their work lives and their personal lives, great businesses know that the whole person comes to work and that each employee's well-being influences individual and organisational performance. Engaged employees, rather than resisting change, will not only help your business, they will lead the way. Engaged workforces turn a business into an agile, responsive force, where innovation and continuous improvement are the norm.

SUMMARY

Transforming your business to be more effective and profitable is not easy. It takes a lot of energy and effort to initiate change, and even more to build on that momentum. During times of transition, active engagement is a powerful tool for motivating employees to adopt change. The most highly engaged organisations do not get that way by accident; it takes proper execution, hard work and perseverance. It is your key to smoothly introducing new ways of thinking and behaving.

The next chapter will introduce the *Adapt Method* – an employee engagement focused approach to managing change in business.

CHAPTER 4

THE ADAPT METHOD

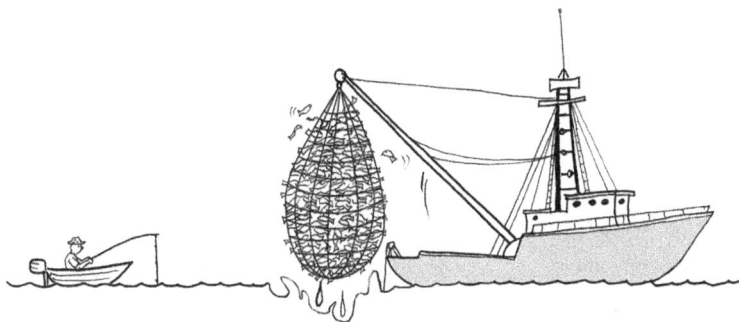

TRULY ADAPTIVE FIRMS WITH ADAPTIVE CULTURES ARE AWESOME COMPETITIVE MACHINES

JOHN P KOTTER – EDUCATOR

Whether you're a franchisee, an entrepreneur, a shop owner or an online service provider, getting to the top of your game has no shortcut. Making mistakes or wasting valuable resources when growing your business, innovating, commercialising products, or making change can cost you dearly. What can also be costly is dealing with resistance and employees opposing the direction you want to take the business.

New employees learn the way your business *currently* works when they first join your company. That is, they will adjust to the *way we do things around here*. When things change, employees must modify their behaviour or learn new skills to suit *new* conditions, needs, or expectations. Employees need to adapt to new circumstances or adjust to new controls or leadership expectations.

This can result in friction and opposition. Employees who feel negatively impacted during a business change can feel resentful and disempowered. Employees need help to adapt to changing circumstances so they can regain confidence and trust in the business and their ability to perform to management's expectations.

The Adapt Method is a roadmap to lead employees through change and back to a place of control of themselves and their working environment. It aims to minimise the pain employees experience and maximise the productivity gains for the business.

BUSINESS CHANGE TYPES

Before introducing the details of the method, it will help to understand the different types of change employees and your business can encounter.

BASIC CHANGE
The most basic type is creating an outcome without having to change the way people work. For example: changing a brand, increasing product pricing, selling an asset to generate cash flow.

MODE OF OPERATION CHANGE
The next type of change is more significant because it requires employees to adjust their behaviour or adopt new methods in line with what they already do in their work today – but

they don't have to change the way they feel about their work or the business. For instance, an employee may be required to store their work electronically rather than create print-outs. Or perhaps they need to send freight items using an online booking system rather than by phone, or follow a re-engineered process that optimises workflow and productivity.

PEOPLE-CENTERED CHANGE

The third and more difficult type of change is when employees are required to adjust not only their behaviour, but also their mindset – the way they think about their work. This includes how employees make decisions, create new ideas, solve problems, assess outcomes, determine associations and links, or, simply put, how they join the dots. It's often referred to as cultural change and has a much deeper impact on the individual person. Here are a few more examples to illustrate: introducing company values that set the standards for how a workforce deals with customer complaints; shifting the attitudes of competitive, autonomous team members to one of kinship and collaboration; urging employees to adopt a customer-centric approach for interacting with clientele; introducing a fully automated system to replace existing processes that requires substantial learning of new skills and requires job roles to be modified.

The approach outlined in this book can be used to manage each of the above change types. If you are dealing with a basic change, your activities need only be light and for a short period. However, if you are embarking on a people-centered change, you will need to implement the approach in detail for a lengthy period to achieve success, getting your workforce to make the deep-down change you seek.

THE ADAPT METHOD

The *Adapt Method* has five stages: **Assess**. **Define**. **Apply**. **Prevent**. **Transfer**. It is a leadership approach to helping employees adjust to changing conditions with less resistance, in less time and with less stress on the business owner driving the change.

This method is designed to take you through a practical and logical system for introducing something new and, more importantly, reap the financial benefits of having managed that change well. It will lead you in what to do, what not to do, and explain why. It will show you how to get your employees on-board and how to create raving supporters of the path you want your business to travel. In addition, the chapters can also be used as references to look up individually during your change process.

Below is an overview of each of the stages, with greater detail provided in the subsequent chapters dedicated to each stage.

STAGE 1 ASSESS

The first stage is about looking into your business to detect people-centred barriers that could prevent the change from being successful.

This is achieved by assessing the change-readiness of your business – judging how open your employees are to accepting change and how quickly they'll bounce back from the impact of change (their resilience to it).

In this stage you will answer three questions:
• Why does your business need to change?
• What is your Change Goal?
• How change-ready are your employees?

Taking time out to reflect on these questions will help to determine how solid your foundations for change are. For instance, you might identify a particular employee or department who will object to the change, so it helps to know that at the earliest stage.

STAGE 2 DEFINE

Here you investigate how the change will impact the existing processes in your business. Then, armed with this information, you will define the activities needed to facilitate and support your business and employees through the transition period. This will set up your changing business for success by minimising activities, not going *according to plan*.

In this stage you will define:
- the impact the change will have on your business
- a Learning Plan
- a Communications Plan
- an Engagement Plan
- a Feedback Plan
- a Support Plan.

STAGE 3 APPLY

The change to your business begins here in earnest. There's a lot of activity going on to implement the change. By applying the plans you have created, you will support employees as they start adapting to the change. This stage of the method supports you, the business leader, through this hectic period.

In this stage you will:
- apply your Learning Plan
- ramp up your Communications Plan and employee engagement to build an atmosphere of trust, openness and sharing
- action your Support Plan.

STAGE 4 PREVENT

This next stage aims to prevent resistance from impacting the change effort. It also provides guidance on eliminating operational obstacles and gathering feedback to improve the adoption of the change across the business.

In this stage you will:
- prevent resistance taking hold by identifying and removing any operational structure or system that may create conflict with the new way of working
- action your Feedback Plan.

STAGE 5 TRANSFER

The final stage focuses on transferring the change into your business to ensure it sticks, that the energy doesn't fizzle, and the *new way of doing business* is anchored into your culture.

In this stage you will:
- take action to ensure the change has transferred into your culture and employees' behaviours
- learn what to do if the change isn't *sticking*.

WHAT ARE THE BENEFITS OF USING THE ADAPT METHOD?

Managing and leading people through change can be a difficult process. There are lots of pitfalls and roadblocks along the way. So is it worth it? That's a fair question, so let's take a moment to understand how consciously managing change will help your business to grow and make life easier.

IT CREATES BUY-IN AND SUPPORT

The *Adapt Method* shows you how to create a compelling Change Goal and communicate it effectively. Buy-in to the change is gained through sharing a Change Goal and generating energy, awareness, and enthusiasm. Employee buy-in results in acceptance of the change and minimises objections and resistance.

A Change Goal is a powerful tool to engage people to align with where you are trying to take your business. When someone buys into a Change Goal, they are buying into the meaning of the change. This generates focus, and guides decision-making. Your Change Goal describes why you want to take the business in this new direction. It communicates the reasons why the change is important, not just to the business, but to every person working in it. It creates a picture of a better, more fruitful future for all.

IT HELPS OVERCOME RESISTANCE

The *Adapt Method* provides techniques to minimise resistance by helping you support employees through the change and out the other side.

People resist change; it is a commonly known phenomenon. Why? Because it takes them out of their comfort zone, it creates stress and causes uncertainty. Change requires us to adjust to shifting conditions, many of which are unknown. At its most extreme it can cause fear and pain.

Imagine yourself in an airplane preparing to parachute-jump for the first time. On the ground, before take-off with the ground firmly under your feet, you feel safe and comfortable. Now, up in the air and bracing yourself to jump, what lies ahead outside that plane door is the unknown … and it's terrifying. Your environment is about to change from being solid underfoot to a state of nothingness. Your heart races, your breath comes in short bursts. You feel afraid.

This response is typical of how a lot of people feel when faced with significant change in their environment. Yet, change is an inevitable part of life, so those who view it with fear tend to spend a lot of energy trying unsuccessfully to avoid it.

IT BUILDS AN APPETITE TO EMBRACE CHANGE

The *Adapt Method* gives you techniques to get your team involved in the process, which in turn builds their investment in the outcome. A powerful way to build an employee's desire to adopt change is to give them an active role in it. Involving employees in the process often turns them into *change champions.*

IT IDENTIFIES OBSTACLES

The *Adapt Method* gives you tools to identify the obstacles in people's minds that prevent them from wanting to embrace change and provides guidance on how to deal with those issues. Despite the best of intentions, new initiatives at work can cause employees to see huge obstacles in their way, even if they aren't really there. Dealing with the barriers your employees see, whether real or perceived, is vital to the success of your business after the change has been implemented.

IT DEFEATS COMPLACENCY

The *Adapt Method* shows you how to communicate effectively, to drive people out of their status quo mindset so you can lead them into new territory. Feeling comfortable with the way things are now can hinder a person's desire to want to change. When employees are feeling complacent, they don't put in the extra effort needed to make the change a success.

IT RALLIES THE TROOPS TOGETHER

The *Adapt Method* shows you how to form a partnership with employees who can help usher in change by generating support, and leading others through it with you. When growing your business, you need your team to rally behind you. Employees with influence can stand up and motivate others to come along on the journey.

IT OFFERS PROOF THAT THINGS ARE CHANGING AROUND HERE

The *Adapt Method* shows you how to highlight visible improvements in process, performance and behaviour.

Demonstrating that change is actually happening for the better is important in order to get the sceptics in your organisation on board. By drawing attention to small improvements, or *wins*, you start to make the change appear real and successful.

IT HIGHLIGHTS THE IMPORTANCE OF CELEBRATING
The *Adapt Method* offers ways to integrate recognition into your day-to-day activities during times of transition. Celebrating the achievement of goals or milestones during the transition is an effective way of keeping employees motivated about the change. Recognition and small rewards help make people feel valued and inspire more effort to keep going.

IT INSTIGATES AND DEALS WITH FEEDBACK
The *Adapt Method* provides you with tools to gather feedback and ways to deal with the insights you receive. Communication builds bridges, while conversation builds relationships and connections. A healthy practice during times of change is to encourage innovative ideas, suggestions and constructive criticism from your employees.

Different people bring different perspectives to the same problem, and allowing open communication about how well things are traveling often gives rise to better solutions. Encouraging feedback also serves to engage employees in the outcome of the change; they will form a deeper connection with the result and its success. Implementing actions based on feedback is a very effective way to improve the outcome of your initiative.

IT ENSURES THE CHANGE STICKS

The *Adapt Method* provides techniques to ensure the change will stick for the long term. Change sticks only when it is firmly anchored into *the way we do things around here*. Unless new behaviour is grounded into what's normal in your business, it is likely that over time people will regress back to old ways of working as soon as the pressure of the transition effort is over.

HOW MUCH TIME AND EFFORT DOES IT TAKE TO APPLY THE ADAPT METHOD?

The answer to that question can be as long as a piece of string or no time at all, depending on the complexity of the change, how ready your business is to cope with the change, and how willing you are to do the work that's required for the change to be a resounding success. However, to illustrate, two examples are provided below.

CASE STUDY: RETAIL BUSINESS WITH 12 STAFF

This small business was entering the next growth stage by introducing a new product range and customer service strategy to support its launch. By applying the *Adapt Method* they were able to assimilate the changes into business-as-usual in two months. The business saw an instant impact to sales figures. Employees were enthusiastic and happy about selling the new products and excited about what other lines the business might be able to introduce down the track.

Stage	Elapsed Timeframe	What did they do?	Effort
Assess	Week 1–2	The business owner created a Change Goal and ran two focus groups to assess their change-readiness.	4 hours
Define	Week 3–4	A Support team of three, from different business functions, was assembled to identify the impacts to their current processes.	3 hours
		The team created a product knowledge and sales skills based Learning Plan and Communications Plan.	3 hours
		The business owner created an Engagement and Feedback Plan.	1 hour
		The business owner defined what support he would need from his Team Supervisor to introduce the changes.	0.5 hours
Apply	Week 4–5	The Support team actioned the Communications Plan.	4 hours over two weeks
		The Support team actioned the Learning Plan.	2 hours x 9 employees
		The business owner took all 12 staff through 3 team-based engagement activities.	2.5 hours

Stage	Elapsed Timeframe	What did they do?	Effort
Prevent	Week 4–6	The business owner ran an online survey to capture feedback and discovered two factors in his operating model that were in conflict with the new sales process.	3 hours
		The Team Supervisor and two senior staff eliminated the obstacles.	2 hours
		The owner and supervisor both spent time meeting with different team members to discuss, encourage and deal with individual concerns regarding the new approach.	5 hours
Transfer	Week 6–8	The owner and supervisor undertook all of the recommended activities in this stage.	7 hours
		To mark the end of the transition, the team were taken on an afternoon lunch cruise together to celebrate their achievements.	3 hours

CASE STUDY: COMMERCIAL BUSINESS WITH 120 STAFF

This medium-sized business was introducing a more sophisticated customer relationship management system. By applying the *Adapt Method* they were able to adopt the technology in three months. The company did not experience a decline in performance and commenced generating a return on their investment on target.

Stage	Elapsed Timeframe	What did they do?	Effort
Assess	Week 1–3	Senior leaders met to create a Change Goal. They ran an online survey to assess all employees change-readiness, and followed up with discussions of the results in team meetings.	8 hours
Define	Week 3–5	Senior leaders, with help from team leaders, identified the impacts to their current processes.	10 hours
		The HR Manager created a Learning Plan, Communications Plan and Engagement Plan.	6 hours
		The HR Manager created a Feedback Plan after consulting with team leaders.	1.5 hours
		Senior leaders defined a Support Plan for employees and team leaders.	2 hours
Apply	Week 4–10	Team leaders actioned the Learning, Communications and Engagement Plans.	15 hours
		Team leaders facilitated practice sessions on a non-live version of the new system with employees in roles that would spend more than 50% of their time using it.	30 minutes x 45 employees

Stage	Elapsed Timeframe	What did they do?	Effort
Prevent	Week 6–10	Senior leaders ran feedback workshops with small groups to hear how teams were planning to get the most out of the new system.	1 hour x 12 groups
		Time was spent dealing with about 10% of staff who were resistant to using the new system.	5 hours
		Incentives were introduced into existing pay scales to entice motivated employees to become super-users.	3 hours
Transfer	Week 9–12	Senior leaders and team leaders undertook numerous activities to reinforce the value to the business of the new system and recognised employees who were using it effectively.	8 hours
		To celebrate the first day the system went live, every employee received a box of chocolates and a movie voucher in appreciation of their contribution. After the first month of use, an award and recognition program was launched to acknowledge employees who were using the system to reach sales targets faster.	3 hours

WHAT CAN YOU ACHIEVE FROM APPLYING THE ADAPT METHOD

The *Adapt Method* provides all the tools needed to be a brilliant leader of change in commercial and retail small to medium business. Applying the techniques helps business owners create an energised, enthusiastic workforce to enable their business to flourish during a transition or growth period.

Here's a rundown of what you can achieve by following the *Adapt Method*.

Stage	What gets done	Why it's important
Assess	The need for change in your business, the readiness of employees and the benefits you can expect are assessed. A Change Goal is created to give the change purpose.	The chances of your business change being successful are greatly enhanced when you take the time to assess why your business needs to change, the benefits of the change, and how change-ready your employees are.
Define	The business processes impacted by the change are identified. Then the Learning, Communications, Engagement, Feedback and Support your business needs to successfully manage the change are defined.	The amount of planning you do to prepare your business for change directly affects how successful the implementation will be.
Apply	The Learning, Communications, Engagement and Support Plans are applied to drive the change into your business.	Old thinking and habits need to be replaced with new ones. Critical to this is delivering learning efficiently, communicating effectively, engaging and supporting your workforce.

Stage	What gets done	Why it's important
Prevent	People-blockers and organisational obstructions that could slow or prevent the change taking effect are identified. Further problems are prevented by actioning the Feedback Plan.	To avoid regression and get the changes to stick it is important to remove any existing system or operational activity that obstructs the change.
Transfer	The change to your business is checked to ensure it has transferred successfully into the culture.	Getting your employees to sustain the change is important. If change is not reinforced properly or not fully anchored into your mode of operation, then behaviour can revert back and the benefits of the change can be lost.

SUMMARY

The *Adapt Method* gives you tools and techniques to significantly increase the chance of your employees embracing a change, making it work, and realising the financial benefits of your investment. By following the steps, you will learn how to engage your employees and have them as committed to making your business succeed as you are. Simply put, the *Adapt Method* considers the people factor – their thoughts, their feelings and their needs in a business context. The end game is to enable your business to flourish.

In the next chapter you will get a chance to put the first stage, Assess, of the *Adapt Method* into action by assessing how prepared your business is to accept change in the current environment.

STAGE 1 ASSESS – YOUR BUSINESS CHANGE-READINESS

TRADITION IS A VERY POWERFUL FORCE

JOHN P KOTTER – EDUCATOR

Taking the time to assess why your business needs to change and if it's ready to make the change you're planning is an important step to managing it well.

In this chapter you will:
• reflect on why you are introducing this workplace change and the outcome or profitable result you are expecting from it

- create a Change Goal – the vision for your business after the change
- dig into the interpersonal environment of your business to assess if employees are ready to embrace the change – or not – by assessing your business's *change-readiness*
- reveal any people-centred barriers that could prevent the change from being successful and remove these initial mind-blockers.

We start this chapter by understanding the business and personal needs for the change so that you can create a Change Goal in the next section.

EXERCISE 5.1: GET CLEAR ON WHY YOUR BUSINESS NEEDS TO CHANGE

The purpose of this exercise is to be able to talk with ease about why the business is transitioning to something new and different.

WHAT TO DO

Read through each question and record your answer in the space provided.

1. Name the change or describe it.

_____

_____

_____

_____

_____

2. Why do you want to change your business? Is it to avoid something negative or to gain something positive? Is it to grow, streamline, expand, etc.? Is it to achieve a specific objective? What are the main reasons?

a

_____

_____

_____

b

_____

_____

_____

c

_____

_____

_____

3. What will happen if you don't introduce this change to your business?

_____

_____

_____

_____

4. What do you want in return for investing time, money and effort into the change? Is it to generate more revenue, increase client numbers, reduce costs, improve productivity, or create a happier workplace? What will the benefit be to you, your employees, and your business?

You:

_____

_____

_____

_____

Employees:

_____

_____

_____

_____

Business:

_____

_____

_____

_____

5. What will your business look like after the change? Imagine the change to have already happened and you are observing your business from afar. How is your business now operating? What are you and your employees doing differently? How do you feel? What has improved?

    Some examples might include things like: more customers or happier customers, more profit or less waste, more time or less stress, etc. What will the future look like after the change has been implemented?

_____

_____

_____

_____

_____

6. Summarise your answers to questions 1 - 5 in a couple of sentences here. You will know you're clear when you can explain in less than two minutes why your business must change, what the benefits are, and what the future looks like.

_____

_____

_____

_____

_____

_____

7. Check that the statement is clear, concise and captures a *picture* of how your business will flourish as a result of the change.

WHAT TO DO NEXT

Before moving onto Exercise 5.2 *Create a Change Goal* read the next section to familiarise yourself with the features of a good Change Goal statement and why it's important to have one.

ABOUT CHANGE GOALS

Communicating a shared purpose – your Change Goal – creates energy and unity between people about the change. A Change Goal creates awareness of what's changing, why it's needed and, when appropriate, the risks of not changing. It is a picture of the future. It tells people: *this is how our world is changing and here are the compelling reasons why we must strive to get there.* It engages people in the journey ahead and helps focus their actions and decisions.

CHARACTERISTICS OF A GOOD CHANGE GOAL STATEMENT

Good Change Goals are easy to understand. They're not so grand that they seem unrealistic or impossible to achieve. They are written in simple language so it's easy for every employee to internalise. They tell what there is to be gained. They describe what the benefits to employees or the business will be. They describe a better state of business, or a better environment to work in, or a better outcome for employees or customers or the community. And they can be judged because they can be measured.

Let's look at five examples of good Change Goals.

Reducing complaints by 12% by eliminating the unnecessary or difficult steps in our application process from the customer's perspective.

Providing customers with a seamless online shopping experience, quick payment methods and fast delivery resulting in a 20% increase in revenue this year.

Increasing collaboration between departments so that more employees have a voice in the decisions made within the company to achieve a 5% increase in employee satisfaction.

Decreasing the production cost by 8% to avoid job losses.

Creating a service request process that can be fully automated online to remove a repetitious, mundane internal process from the Contact Centre.

Creating a clear Change Goal takes time, thought, and sometimes even soul searching. The most important question your Change Goal statement needs to answer is what your employees will want to know most – the *what's in it for me?* It should give employees hope that your business is striving for something better. Otherwise, it is difficult for them to let go of being comfortable in the now and be willing to embrace the uncomfortable feeling of the future.

A demonstration of this using the previous Change Goal examples would be:
- Fewer complaints for employees to deal with and therefore less stress.
- Less complicated processes that take less time to administer.
- Empowering of employees to voice their opinions.
- Safeguarding jobs.
- Reducing the amount of boring, mundane or routine tasks in the Customer Contact Centre.

Now let's take a look at a sample of poorly written Change Goals.

To create the next generation of our app to please customers and achieve financial success.

To develop a diverse set of scalable and strategic knowledge management tools.

To be the most successful web design company in Australia.

In summary, a good Change Goal:
- is clear and easy to understand
- is written in simple language
- is measurable
- describes the benefits of the change
- describes the business or work environment after the change has taken place.

Once you have created a clear Change Goal, every conversation, decision and action can be judged against it. It keeps people on track, focused and empowered to reject any activity that doesn't align with it. Having a Change Goal gives people clarity and comfort about the new situation. A strong Change Goal motivates people by making clear that the benefits of the change will result in something more desirable than what they have today.

CASE STUDY: REDUCTION IN SERVICES

A not-for-profit charity needed to reduce their operating costs and decided to reduce the number of services they offered rather than cut jobs. Management knew that employees would react negatively to the news because they valued the community services that were to be withdrawn. Had the change been announced simply as an operational cost-cutting exercise, employees would have been immediately resistant, reducing the charity's ability to achieve the desired outcome. Instead, management created a Change Goal that positioned it as enabling employees to improve the way they served the community. This meant fewer services were offered, but there was more time to have meaningful interactions with clients. Clarifying the benefit to employees and involving them in creating the measurable outcome of the Change Goal resulted in low employee resistance, more willingness to apply the change, and greater persistence whenever the transition to the new way of working became momentarily problematic.

EXERCISE 5.2: CREATE A CHANGE GOAL

The purpose of this exercise is to write a clear, concise Change Goal that will be meaningful to your workforce about the benefits and opportunities the change will bring to the future of your business and their jobs.

WHAT TO DO

Read through each question and record your answer in the space provided. For a free downloadable version of this template, go to *www.adaptusconsulting.com.au*

1. Bring together small groups of employees from different roles and seniority levels across your business to help you craft the goal.

2. Brainstorm ideas to come up with a phrase or sentence using each of these prompts:

The problem we're trying to fix is:

_____

_____

_____

The result we're trying to achieve is:

_____

_____

_____

The benefits to the business, employees, customers, and/or community are:

_____

_____

_____

We will measure the success of the change by:

_____

_____

_____

Our future looks like:

_____

_____

_____

3. Write the ideas on a whiteboard so you can easily modify them as the conversation progresses.

4. Using what you've captured, create one sentence that covers all the points in question 2. Generalising and using vague, feel-good, sweeping statements that don't mean anything won't interest people. Statements like: *We will be the best, Our employees will thrive,* or *Our product will be world class* are examples of poor phrases.

_____

_____

_____

5. Once you have a draft, ask each member of the group to take it and share it with their colleagues back on the job for feedback on its clarity and meaningfulness.

6. Suggest they ask their team or colleagues these questions to check the effectiveness of the goal. For example:
   • Does it make sense?
   • Does it sound credible?
   • Does it answer the *What's in it for me?* question?
   • Do they understand the problem being fixed, or the positive result of the change?
   • What new opportunities does the Change Goal suggest to them?
   • Can they picture the future?

7. Re-convene the intitial group. Discuss the feedback and refine the statement.

8. When the group agrees that it's clear, realistic, and compelling, you can consider it done.

9. Print it out and post it around your office or premises to demonstrate to employees that the Change Goal has been decided and being implemented.

10. Now start talking about the Change Goal at every opportunity, meeting, conversation and interaction. Make the Change Goal a part of your business's DNA by repeating it in some form every day. That way, your employees will start to feel the change that is coming is real and worthwhile. *How?* Because the Change Goal tells them so!

WHAT TO DO NEXT
The more your employees hear about the change, the more they will want to be a part of it. The next exercise will help you to engage a broader range of employees by introducing the Change Goal and spreading the message across your whole workforce.

EXERCISE 5.3: ENGAGE EMPLOYEES OF INFLUENCE TO SHARE THE CHANGE GOAL
Employees who hear information from well-respected leaders, their immediate line manager, or trusted fellow workmates will believe in it more than if it only comes from you (e.g. CEO, business owner, etc.). So take advantage of this. The purpose of this exercise is to mobilise employees of influence to share the Change Goal with other employees so everyone is across where the business is going.

WHAT TO DO

1. Identify trusted workers or highly regarded employees in your business.

2. Ask them to take personal responsibility for sharing the Change Goal with as many employees as possible in as many conversations as possible.

3. Encourage them to talk about how their team or their workmates can contribute to making the Change Goal successful. Often these conversations will cause people who are unsupportive of the change to speak out. This is a good way of sussing out if there are any early resistors.

WHAT TO DO NEXT

If you recognise any employees pushing back or rejecting the Change Goal, then read the next section, *Early resistance – how does it start?*, and go onto completing Exercise 5.4. Or, if you are satisfied that all employees are on board at this stage, read the section, *Being change-ready is the foundation for success*, and complete Exercise 5.5 to start assessing how change-ready your business is.

EARLY RESISTANCE – HOW DOES IT START?

It is common to encounter some resistance in the early days of managing a change. Typically early signs of resistance will come from employees who are comfortable and deeply invested in the *way we do things around here*. Or from those who are disengaged from your business, culture or values.

There are many reasons for early resistance. Here are some of the common ones:

- Employees have worked this way for many years and have become comfortable with the status quo.
- Employees fear change because they don't feel confident about learning new skills.
- Employees don't believe there is a need to change and discredit the reasons presented.
- Employees are already complacent and only want to do the bare minimum required; making a change requires effort.
- Employees may just be plain unwilling to change because they feel it's their right to keep doing what they've always done, creating a *can't teach an old dog new tricks* kind of attitude.

EXERCISE 5.4: DEAL WITH EARLY RESISTORS

The purpose of this exercise is to nip early resistance in the bud. It is wise to deal with employees who oppose change as soon as it surfaces. Dealing with employees using the guidelines in this exercise will reduce the likelihood of resistance persisting at the beginning of a transition and help to engage them directly in the change at the same time.

WHAT TO DO

1. Set up a one-on-one meeting in a café or in a park, or away from the normal place of work to create a neutral setting.

2. Ask them to explain the issue they have and why they feel the way they do.

3. Respond to their objections with understanding, empathy and firmness. Here are some points you might cover:

   - Why does the business need to change? This must not be something vague like, *We need to make more sales*, or *We need to diversify*. People need to know what the risk is to the business of not making the change.
   - What are the goals of the change?
   - How will the change impact them in a positive way – their job, role, workload, responsibilities, accountabilities, decision-making and environment?
   - How does the change benefit them personally and professionally? Answer the question, *What's in it for me?*
   - Why does it have to be now and not later? Find something that resonates with them personally: if the business doesn't change there will be less jobs, fewer promotions, no surplus for training, less budget for Christmas parties, etc.
   - Why was this solution chosen?
   - Why do you need their help to make it happen?

4. Show them evidence of what you claim, with charts, graphs or reports that demonstrate what's not working. In other words, the reason for the change. For example, showing evidence of a reduction in performance, a decline in sales, or growing debt figures is a good way to get people's attention.

5. After the meeting, check-in with them personally on at least two further occasions to ensure they understand the necessity and importance of the business implementing the change and to answer other questions they may have.

6. If the resistance persists, refer to Chapter 15 *Dealing with Resistance* for ways to take further action.

WHAT TO DO NEXT

Make the effort to spend time with resistors. Everything that affects them must be communicated upfront. If you are satisfied that the early resistors are now more supportive of the Change Goal, then read the next section and complete Exercise 5.5 to assess how change-ready your business is.

BEING CHANGE-READY IS THE FOUNDATION FOR SUCCESS

Checking that your workforce is change-ready is important because it tells you how prepared your business is to deal with what's to come. Change requires everyone to make an effort and contribute in some form. Think of it like a team sport. Every player needs to be fully focused on doing his or her best to win the game. Problems arise when some of the team don't play by the rules or don't try hard enough, leaving those who play their best to try to win the game alone and unsupported.

Change-ready teams *want to* change rather than *have to* change. Determining your business's change-readiness is about judging how open your employees' hearts and minds are to accepting a change. Being change-ready is important as it indicates that your team will support the change, and also that they believe your business is capable of implementing the change successfully.

Change management experts say that greater readiness leads to more successful change implementation. But how, or why, is this so?

When change-readiness is high, people are more inclined to give the extra effort that's needed, persist when faced with obstacles or setbacks, and behave more co-operatively. Although a high level of change-readiness does not *guarantee* that the change to your business will succeed, it does set it up for success.

CASE STUDY: THE CHANGE-READINESS IMPACT

A small Australian bank was trying to adopt a new set of government regulations into their day-to-day operations. Unfortunately they didn't check if their business or people were change-ready. They didn't take the time to find out if their workforce was in a frame of mind to accept the new changes to their processes. Instead they forged ahead and rolled out the new regulations and expected employees to enforce them. But they didn't. Many employees didn't understand the new regulations or ignored them completely believing they had better judgment than the regulators. The change was considered a failure and a lot of corrective action, time and effort went into overcoming the resistance and getting the change implemented into business-as-usual.

BENEFITS OF TESTING YOUR BUSINESS'S CHANGE-READINESS

The benefit of checking-in before your business change commences is significant. Surveying for change-readiness opens the door for you to better understand how your employees feel and think about what's about to happen. And it provides the opportunity to prevent resistance taking hold from the beginning. It also starts lots of engaging conversations and reinforces the key messages of the change. It gets people thinking about their role in the change and makes real that something different is about to happen.

Change-readiness can be tested. Done well, the results and insights will tell you how, when and where you need to intervene to improve the success of your business change. Two approaches are outlined below, one using conversation, the other using a survey. Face-to-face discussions are beneficial if you only have a few employees and if trust and camaraderie exists between them. Surveys are useful if you need to reach a large group of employees, or if they are in different locations, or if employees are uncomfortable with openly expressing their views.

EXERCISE 5.5: ASSESS HOW CHANGE-READY YOUR BUSINESS IS

The purpose of this exercise is to look more deeply into your workplace culture to assess how willing and able your employees are to accept the impact of the change. This exercise helps to engage employees further by talking openly about their involvement in the change, and to create awareness and enthusiasm about how and why their environment is going to change. Assessing your business's change-readiness will help your project be successful.

WHAT TO DO

First, you need to decide how to assess your business's change-readiness. Although there are many techniques available, it is highly recommended small to medium companies choose one of the following options. Decide which approach suits your culture best, or combine the two.

Option	Description	Recommendation For	Exercise
Focus Groups	This technique uses interactive conversation in small groups to assess change-readiness.	Micro or small businesses with fewer than 25 employees.	Complete Exercise 5.5a
Survey	This technique uses a survey to assess change-readiness.	For leaders who are time poor or businesses with more than 25 employees.	Complete Exercise 5.5b

EXERCISE 5.5A: ASSESSING CHANGE-READINESS USING FOCUS GROUPS

1. Set up meetings with no more than 10 employees at a time.

2. Re-introduce the Change Goal:
   • Explain the decisions that have been made so far.
   • Describe what action has taken place to get things started.
   • Paint a picture of the end result and its benefits to reinforce the value you are expecting out of the change.
   • Describe what role the group will play in helping to facilitate the change.
   • Explain the process the business will go through to deploy the change.

3. Select from the sample of questions below or create your own to test employees' state of change-readiness.

- Why is the change needed?
- How will this change help our business to flourish?
- How will the change have a positive impact on you, your job, our business, your colleagues, our customers and our community?
- How should we deal with obstacles?
- What contribution does your team need to make to help the business undertake the change?
- What role will *you, the employee,* play in the change?
- What new skills and knowledge do you need to adopt the new way of working?
- What support do you need?
- Do you think management can lead this change successfully? If not, what do they need to improve?
- What ideas do you have for how we could use the increased revenue, time, opportunity, etc. to improve the future of our business and your team or job?
- Is our business ready for the change and can we pull together to make it a success?

4. Invite employees to comment, raise concerns, and offer ideas to improve the approach.

5. Document concerns or issues that have been raised.

6. Ask participants for ideas to solve the problems shared in the session. Often, employees will know the answer themselves.

If there are questions you cannot answer, or a resolution is not clear or requires a management decision, offer to come back to the group with a response.

7. Share the concerns and solutions with other groups attending change-readiness focus groups.

8. Repeat this exercise with the next group.

EXERCISE 5.5B: ASSESSING CHANGE-READINESS USING A SURVEY

1. Give a copy of **Template 5.1: Is our business ready to change?** to each employee. For a free downloadable version of this template, go to *www.adaptusconsulting.com.au*

2. Ask them to complete it in a specific timeframe (e.g. 2 days, during a meeting, over the weekend, etc.).

3. Reassure employees that their responses will be used to help you understand their concerns and where they need support.

4. Once you have received back all the surveys, calculate the scores and collate the comments people have made. by following the *Change-readiness Scoresheet* section of this chapter. How did your business rate its change-readiness?

5. Arrange a meeting to allow employees to discuss the results with you. Highlight areas that were found to have high and low results.

6. Encourage employees to ask questions and air their concerns. Treat these issues sensitively, and take on board any actions agreed at the meeting. Be sure to follow through. That's how you build trust and credibility. Explain how you are going to overcome the areas that scored low.

WHAT TO DO NEXT

Now that you have a good understanding of how prepared and open your employees are to accepting the change to come, you can move on to the next stage.

TEMPLATE 5.1: IS OUR BUSINESS READY TO CHANGE?

Please mark your response with an X for each statement.

Is our business ready to change?	Yes	No	Unsure	Comment on why you feel that way
1. I understand why the business needs to [change].				
2. I agree with the [change] that is coming.				
3. I think there are benefits to me /our business / my colleagues / our customers / our community in making the [change].				
4. I believe our business can successfully implement the [change].				
5. I am confident our business can overcome any obstacles to making the [change] a success.				
6. I believe I have the energy and the will to help make the [change] a success.				
7. I believe employees will be supported through the [change].				
8. I believe I will be given the opportunity to be involved in the [change] and to learn new skills and knowledge to adopt the new way of working.				
9. I am confident that management can lead the [change] successfully.				
10. I believe our culture will positively support the [change].				
11. I believe our business will become more prosperous if we make the [change].				
12. I believe our business is ready for the [change] and will pull together to make it a success.				

CHANGE-READINESS SCORESHEET

1	2	3	4	5	6	7	8	9	10	11	12
Poor change-readiness				Satisfactory change-readiness				High change-readiness			

HOW TO SCORE ONE PERSON INDIVIDUALLY

Each question earns one point when a box is marked in the *Yes* column.

Example: A participant marks *Yes* to 5 questions, marks *No* to 6 questions, and marks 1 question as *I'm unsure*. The person's total score will equal 5 points putting them in the *Satisfactory change-readiness* category but close to the *Poor change-readiness* category. You will need to examine their comments to understand why this is so.

HOW TO SCORE A GROUP

Score each survey individually. Then tally up the scores of all the participants. Does the average of the total scores sit within the Poor, Satisfactory or High range? Once you know, follow the feedback given in the relevant category below.

HIGH CHANGE-READINESS: Total average score is between 9 and 12

Well done! Your business is at a high level of readiness. Keep doing what you're doing. You're on the right track to making the change a success. Share this news with your team. Congratulate them on being change-ready. Show your appreciation for their willingness to get on board with where your business wants to go.

SATISFACTORY CHANGE-READINESS: Total average score is between 5 and 8

Your business is at a satisfactory level of readiness. To strengthen it you need to:

1. Continue to have lots of engaging conversations that reinforce the Change Goal.

2. Get employees thinking about their role in the change.

3. Check that employees:
   - believe the change is urgently required to stop something negative happening
   - understand the change will solve an important problem
   - understand how the change will benefit the business, customers and their role
   - agree that the change aligns with the company's core values
   - value the change and the proposed solution.

POOR CHANGE-READINESS: Total average score is between 1 and 4

Your business is at risk of the change being a failure. You need to:

1. Convene small group or one-on-one meetings with employees to tease out the issues.

2. Identify the reasons why employees feel unable to embrace the change coming into your business.

3. Ask these sample questions and your own to get to the heart of what's holding them back:
   - Do you agree with the change? If not, why?
   - What issues or obstacles do you think exist?
   - Why do you feel unable to embrace the change?
   - What support do you need to feel able to adapt?

4. Once the problems have been identified you will need to fix them.

5. Check in with employees in one month's time to assess whether their change-readiness has improved. If not, you need to search again for the root cause and remedy it.

SUMMARY

- Creating a Change Goal communicates a shared purpose and helps to build trust in the change.
- A Change Goal that is shared by well-respected and trusted leaders is viewed as more credible than if delivered by just one senior person in the business.
- Conducting a survey to check the change-readiness of your workforce highlights issues and misunderstandings that may prevent the change from being a success.
- When change-readiness is high, people are more inclined to give the extra effort that's needed, persist when faced with obstacles or setbacks, and behave more co-operatively.

STAGE 2 DEFINE – THE IMPACTS TO YOUR BUSINESS

THERE IS NOTHING PERMANENT EXCEPT CHANGE

HERACLITUS – PHILOSPHER

In the next stage of the *Adapt Method*, you will use your Change Goal and insight to define and plan how to roll out the change across your business.

Business author Alan Lakein coined the phrase *Failing to plan is planning to fail*. This phrase is often stated in business contexts to encourage people to make planning a priority. When it comes to managing change well, planning is essential.

Imagine building a house without a plan. How would your builder keep track of the hundreds of small jobs that need to be done? It would be impossible. You'd end up with a house that looked nothing like the one the architect designed and most likely with lots of flaws. It's very easy for problems to occur when there is no planning.

The effort you put into getting ready directly affects how successful your implementation will be and reduces the potential to waste time and effort on activities that are of no, or low, value to the outcome.

A good planner not only decides what needs to be done, but also how, who and when. Planning is critical to making a change work in your business. You need to think about how you are going to get from where you are now to where you want to be. A well-designed plan will make getting there much easier. Don't be tempted to skip this stage because the time you spend now will be a lot less than the time you'll need to fix things up when they *don't go according to plan*.

CASE STUDY: THE HEADACHE OF FORGING AHEAD WITH NO PLAN

A large warehousing company invested in a multi-million dollar IT inventory system. The people responsible for the project considered managing the change much less important than *getting the job done*. Technical teams ploughed ahead customising the solution for the new way the business was going to operate. No time was allowed to understand how different jobs would be impacted. No one considered what new knowledge and skills different employees would need to be able to work the new system effectively. No one told employees what was happening during the change-over period. Consequently, after the old system was switched off and the new one switched on, there was a lot of resistance. Many employees were confused and annoyed at how poorly the transition was managed. For a time the business ground to a halt because they couldn't release goods from the warehouse. Revenue declined, customers were frustrated and the business owners were stressed. A lot of time was spent getting employees using the new system effectively.

Don't make the same mistake. Take the time to plan how you will manage change in your business and avoid the headaches.

In order to know what activities to plan, you must first assess how your business processes will be *impacted* by the change. An *impact* is when a business process can no longer be performed in exactly the same way after the change as it was before the change.

In this chapter you will define how the change will impact your business processes.

EXERCISE 6.1: IDENTIFY IMPACTS TO EXISTING BUSINESS PROCESSES

The purpose of this exercise is to assess which of your operational processes will be affected by the change and to record *what*, *how* and *who* will be affected by the change.

WHAT TO DO

1. Complete **Template 6.1: Identifying Process Impacts**. Here is an example of what a completed template looks like.

Follow the instructions below on how to complete yours. For a free downloadable version of this template, go to *www.adaptusconsulting.com.au*

Section A	Section B	Section C	Section D	Section E	Section F		
General Impact Description	Job / Role Impacted	Skill Impact	Knowledge Impact	Human Resources / Admin Impact	Responsible Person		
					Owner	Approver	Due Date

Row 1 **Process name:** *Safety Maintenance Notification Process*
Row 2 **Description:** *A process to notify personnel of safety hazards and equipment faults*

A new Create Maintenance Notification form needs to be added to the process. The Create Maintenance Ticket is no longer required.	OH&S Officers	OH&S Officers will need to learn how to complete a Create Maintenance Notification form.	OH&S Officers will need to know when to complete the form.	Add task to Safety section of all OH&S Officer job descriptions.	John S – training Sarah B – job role descriptions	Martha T, OH&S Manager	Monday 17th June

2. In **Row 1**, name a process in your business that will be affected by the change, no matter how small the impact may first appear. Small impacts in one process can lead to more significant impacts in other processes. An impact can result in a process or task needing to be revised, or removed altogether, or a new process or task to be created. Use of the term "process" here means any work activity that is being impacted by change.

3. In **Row 2**, describe the purpose of the process.

4. In **Section A**, record what needs to be added, removed or modified in the process – this is the impact to the process caused by the change being introduced.

5. In **Section B**, record which job roles will be affected by the change to this process.

6. In **Section C**, record what employees need to be able to *do* to perform effectively after the change has been made to the process.

7. In **Section D**, record what employees need to *know* to perform effectively.

8. Sometimes change introduces impacts to HR or administrative areas of the business. In **Section E**, capture these impacts.

9. In **Section F**, record:
   a. Who is responsible for making the change to that process?
   b. Who will approve the change (if necessary)?
   c. By what date should the change be implemented?

10. Now repeat steps 2 – 9 for each process in your business that will be impacted by the change.

WHAT TO DO NEXT

By now you will understand how the change will affect your existing business processes. You will also be aware of the new skills and knowledge employees who perform those processes will need to acquire. This work is the preparation needed to create an effective Learning Plan, which is the focus of the next chapter.

TEMPLATE 6.1: IDENTIFYING PROCESS IMPACTS

General Impact Description	Job / Role Impacted	Skill Impact	Knowledge Impact	Human Resources / Admin Impact	Responsible Person		Due Date
					Owner	Approver	
What is changing? What is no longer required?	Which jobs or roles will be impacted?	What new skills or behaviour is required?	What new knowledge is required?	What is the impact to HR or administration?	Who is responsible for making the changes?	Who will approve the changes?	When does it need to be done by?
Process Name: *Description:*							
Process Name: *Description:*							
Process Name: *Description:*							

CHAPTER 7

STAGE 2 DEFINE – WHAT EMPLOYEES NEED TO LEARN

IF YOU CHANGE THE WAY YOU LOOK AT THINGS, THE THINGS YOU LOOK AT CHANGE

WAYNE DYER – PSYCHOLOGIST

Every time you make a change to your business, employees need to learn or alter something – new skills, new knowledge, new abilities. Employees who are confused or lack support don't perform well. They need to have the right expertise before they can competently change-over to something different to ensure their performance levels don't drop.

In this chapter you will create a Learning Plan so your employees will perform successfully after the change.

The aim of a Learning Plan is to define learning activities so your employees can acquire new knowledge and skill. Not everyone learns well in a class or group environment. Be mindful that your employees may need multiple opportunities or a specific learning context to acquire new behaviours. For example, some employees may be dyslexic, some cannot read at all, and some have been out of the education system for twenty years. Those people need to be identified very early on and strategies developed to include them.

With the impacts to your business understood, your role now is to assess what the gaps are between each person and the change, to determine what learning activity is best for them and how much time they need to practise to master the new skills back on the job. Practice is an important consideration when building your Learning Plan. Employees must be allowed to practise newly acquired skills in their own working environment to ensure that the changed behaviour becomes a *habit*.

EXERCISE 7.1: CREATE A LEARNING PLAN

The purpose of this exercise is to:
- document *what* needs to be learned and *how* it can be taught
- define the environment needed for the learning to take place
- identify the practice needed to ensure an employee's attempt at learning is successful.

WHAT TO DO

1. Have a copy of your process and task impacts from the previous exercise ready to refer to.

2. Complete **Template 7.1: Learning Plan**. Here is an example of what a completed template looks like. Follow the instructions below on how to complete yours. For a free downloadable version of this template, go to *www. adaptusconsulting.com.au*

Section A	Section B	Section C	Section D		Section E					Section F
Learning Objective	Audience	Learning Approach	Logistics	Time	Cost	Organiser	Trainer	Resources	Date	Practice Session
Impact: Create Maintenance Notification form										
Develop the skill required to complete a Create Maintenance Notification form & know when it must be completed	OH&S Officers	30 min instruction session	Meeting room Data projector	30 min sessions x 4 45 employees 22.5 hours	Training materials $400	Claire M	Peter S	Instruction sheet to be given to each employee	Monday 10th June	As incidents arise the OH&S Officer is to complete the new form in front of a Supervisor for guidance & checking

3. In the **Impact** row, record the name of an impacted process (refer to Exercise 6.1).

4. In **Section A**, describe the knowledge and/or skill that employees need to be able to perform the changed process – this becomes the objective of the learning activity.

5. In **Section B**, record the specific job roles that need to complete the learning activity.

6. In **Section C**, describe *how* employees will learn the new knowledge or skills. For examples of different types of learning activities, refer below.

Learning Activities

Here are some examples of learning activities you can include in a Learning Plan:

- On-the-job coaching
- Checklists
- Training sessions
- Buddying people up to work a process through whilst helping each other perfect the steps
- Visiting other businesses that have implemented the same change and observing them working
- Watching instructional videos
- Using the new system or equipment in an environment that is not 'live' where they can play and try things out without the fear of damaging something or making a mistake
- Challenging people to work out a better way to complete a task even when they know how the new task can be completed
- Getting a team together to role play or simulate the new activity and give each other feedback on how well they performed
- Assigning early adopters of the change to others who are starting out on their learning journey to provide coaching and assistance
- Getting an individual, who has become an 'expert', to create a set of instructions or a job aid that can be used by their peers back on-the-job to learn the new activity.

Another important consideration is whether employees will need to change their thinking or their attitudes toward something. It's not always enough to just provide skills training. Some change requires employees to make a change to their mindset. One-on-one conversations, encouragement and positive reinforcement assist when dealing with attitudinal change.

7. In **Section D,** record:

    a. The logistics of the training session or learning activity.

    b. The time required to complete the training. For examples of resources you can use in your training, refer below.

Resources

Providing training and learning resources needs organising. You need to find the right instructors, provide facilities, and plan how to cover people while they are attending a learning activity.

Here are some examples of resources you can include in a Learning Plan:
- External professional expert who can run classroom-style training
- Internal instructor to show people how to do things directly on-the-job
- Books, written manuals, How-to ... sheets, checklists, posters, diagrams, templates, DVDs, games, quizzes
- Demonstration equipment
- Knowledge or skill tests
- Non-live systems to learn and practise new skills with.

---

8. In **Section E** record:

    a. What is the cost of the training?

    b. Who will deliver the learning session?

    c. What tools or resources are needed?

    d. What is the date of the training?

9. In **Section F,** record how employees will practise their new skills back on the job. The more often employees can practise their new knowledge and skills, the sooner they will perfect the new way to work.

10. Now repeat steps 3 – 9 for each process or task impacted by the change being introduced into your business.

WHAT TO DO NEXT

Once you have defined the Learning Plan activities, the next step is to plan what communication is required, when it will be required and for whom. Creating a Communications Plan is the focus of the next chapter.

TEMPLATE 7.1: LEARNING PLAN

Learning Objective	Audience	Learning Approach	Logistics	Time	Cost	Organiser	Trainer	Resources	Date	Practice Session
What needs to be learned?	*Who needs to learn it?*	*How will people learn the new behaviour?*	*What venue or equipment is required?*	*What is the time commitment?*	*What is the cost?*	*Who will arrange the learning resources?*	*Who will deliver the learning session?*	*What tools or resources are needed?*	*When will it be delivered?*	*What practice do they need back on the job?*
Impact										
Impact										
Impact										
Impact										
Impact										
Impact										
Impact										

STAGE 2 DEFINE – WHAT EMPLOYEES NEED TO KNOW

THE SINGLE BIGGEST PROBLEM IN COMMUNICATION IS THE ILLUSION IT HAS TAKEN PLACE

GEORGE BERNARD SHAW – DRAMATIST

When it comes to change in the workplace, there is no such thing as too much communication. There is a clear link between good communication and businesses that manage change successfully. If you communicate well, your chances of employees adopting change quickly are much higher.

Employees need to feel that they have a degree of control over the changes that are impacting them. They need to know that their jobs will be both satisfying and challenging after the change has taken place. Communication is a tool to help achieve this.

In this chapter you will create a Communications Plan. There are many different ways to communicate and equally as many messages that need to be shared with employees who are impacted by change. Messages rarely sink in the first time they're heard. You need to repeat them, and often. Communication needs to be delivered in different ways to make sure the correct message gets across. Different people hear different information from the same message, and you need to try to account for this. It's better to communicate precisely, creatively and frequently.

SAME SOUNDING WORDS, DIFFERENT MEANINGS

It's easy for information to be misunderstood. Just because you've given out a communication doesn't mean everybody has heard the same message.

Here are some examples of misunderstandings – same sounding words, different meanings – to emphasise this point:

- Manager says: *What you have seen this last year is a good example of management in action.*
  Employees hear: *What we saw was management inaction!*
- Manager says: *Our meetings will be bimonthly.* [Meaning every two months.]
  Employees hear: *Meetings will be twice a month.*

PRINCIPLES OF GOOD COMMUNICATION

Before we go through the subjects that are important to consider when planning good communication, let's focus for a minute on three important principles:

1. **Keep it simple** – when you communicate, it can't be complicated, clumsy or wordy. It's important to not be technical or full of jargon.

2. **Be clear** – don't ramble or try to talk about too much in one go. One communication should cover one key message. Don't make things difficult for your employees to digest.

3. **Deliver the message in multiple ways** – use examples, analogies, metaphors, quotes, and humour. In other words, use different ways to convey the key message other than just using a statement.

CONSIDERATIONS WHEN PLANNING GOOD COMMUNICATION

Important points to consider when planning your communications are:

- **Audience** – *Who* am I talking to? Communicating is only effective if it's to the right employees. The message to your management team might be different to the sales team and different again to the administration team.
- **Message** – *What* should I tell them? For employees who are only slightly affected by the change, your message may be quite broad and general. But for employees who you will rely on to make the change work, you will need to tell them about different things at different times.
- **Channels** – *How* will I tell them? A communication channel is a means through which a message is transmitted to its intended audience, such as email or face-to-face.

When choosing a channel to send a message, it needs to fit the audience and the type of message you're spreading. You may decide to send general information in an email, but conduct a team meeting to talk about strategy, and use a one-on-one approach to discuss more sensitive issues like job impacts.

- **Timing** – *When* should I tell them? Communicating at the right time is more meaningful. It could be beneficial to convey some messages to your management team first, and then the rest of your employees later. Or if jobs are affected, you may talk to just the leader of the team concerned, and later to everyone else.

WHAT WILL HAPPEN IF I DON'T BOTHER?

So what happens if you don't communicate? You will probably end up in a situation where the people who *shout the loudest* will get heard. Incorrect messages and information can create resistance very fast. In order to avoid having to deal with resistance, it's much easier to tell people everything they need to know. To sum it up, it's not just about what you're saying, it's also about making your message suitable to the audience, delivering it at the right time, and using the right method.

EXERCISE 8.1: CREATE A COMMUNICATIONS PLAN

The purpose of this exercise is to plan out all the communications that need to be issued during the change-over period. Previously you developed a Change Goal statement and shared that with your team. This was the first stage of the communication process. But there's more to do to see the process through, and that is what we will plan for here.

WHAT TO DO

1. Make a list of all the information you can think of that employees, teams, departments, team leaders, senior leaders, etc. will need to know during the change period.

2. Complete **Template 8.1: Communications Plan**. It is a good idea to have a basic communication plan in place to convey general topics to your workforce. Listing the topics can let you keep an eye on what communications need to go out and when. Keep in mind, too, that messages will change-over time and new messages may need to be included in your plan down the track.

   Here is an example of what a completed template looks like. Follow the instructions below on how to complete yours. For a free downloadable version of this template, go to *www.adaptusconsulting.com.au*

Section A	Section B	Section C			Section D	Section E	
Communication Type	Message	Audience			Cost	Responsibility	
		Who	How	When		Author	Approver
Training alert	OH&S Officers must attend the new Create Maintenance Notification training. Speak to your Supervisor to book a session. Training must be completed by Monday 17th June	OH&S Officers and their supervisors	Poster	Tuesday 11th June	$40 (printing)	Sally T	Jenny F

3. In **Section A**, record the reason for the message or type of communication. For examples of typical messages you need to give employees, refer below.

Common Messages

Here are examples of communications you might include in your plan:
- The Change Goal
- The dates the change period is scheduled to begin and expected to end
- An overview of the process the business will undergo to apply the change
- When, what and how training or learning will be managed
- Who to go to with questions or concerns
- Who to go to for technical support
- What other support is available
- How the change is progressing
- What feedback has been received and the action being taken
- What special assistance, support or monitoring is going to be needed on change-over day
- Your job is changing
- Your role is no longer required
- This system, process, policy or procedure is changing or being phased out
- This is the new process
- This is the new behaviour we expect
- This is the new method for thinking about a problem, or approach to dealing with customers, or way of selling our product, etc.
- These are the new activities, responsibilities, outcomes expected from your role or your team
- Departments are being amalgamated, or a team is being moved into another Division, or a newly acquired business is being merged into our existing business.

4. In **Section B**, describe the message and the main points to be conveyed.

5. In **Section C**, record:
   a. Who is the message for?
   b. How you will convey the message?
   c. What date is the message to be delivered?

For examples of different channels you can use to communicate, refer below.

Communication Channels

When planning your communications, you need to determine in what form, or by what means you will deliver the message. The channel needs to match how the audience will want to *hear* or receive the message.

Communication channel examples are:
- Email
- Letter
- Face-to-face conversation
- Group meeting
- Video
- Company website
- Poster
- Newsletter
- Over a loudspeaker
- Phone call
- Skype or Google hangout
- Formal presentation
- At a conference
- Conducting a site visit.

---

6. In **Section D**, if relevant, record the cost to delivering the communication.

7. In **Section E**, record the details of:
   a. Who is responsible for creating the communication?
   b. Who needs to approve it?

8. Now repeat steps 3 – 7 for each communication in your list

WHAT TO DO NEXT

Once you have planned what you need to tell employees, you are ready to define activities that will inspire and engage your workforce in the change. Creating an Engagement Plan is the focus of the next chapter.

TEMPLATE 8.1: COMMUNICATIONS PLAN

| Communication Type | Message | Audience | | When | Cost | Responsibility | |
		Who	How			Author	Approver
What is the message about?	Main points to be covered in the message	Who will receive the message?	What channel will be used?	When will they receive it?	What costs are involved?	Who will create the communication?	Who will approve it?

STAGE 2 DEFINE – HOW EMPLOYEES WILL BE ENGAGED

> STOP LAUGHING !
> IT HELPS ME FEEL
> EMPOWERED !

YOU HAVE TO ENABLE AND EMPOWER YOUR PEOPLE TO MAKE DECISIONS INDEPENDENT OF YOU. IF THEY FEEL EMPOWERED BY YOU THEY WILL MAGNIFY YOUR POWER TO LEAD

TOM RIDGE – POLITICIAN

If employees are not engaged in the change process, they can get discouraged when something goes wrong or becomes hard. Disengaged employees aren't willing to go the extra mile and are less motivated to learn. Now is the time to plan how to get your team on board with where you are trying to lead your business and the changes that will get you there.

In this chapter you will create an Engagement Plan. An Engagement Plan is a tool to capture the activities and events that will get people tuned-in and keen to participate in the change. Employees with poor attitudes can slow down the progress of change and have a negative effect on the employees around them. Poor attitude costs additional time, effort and money to turn around. Make a plan to address attitude problems now before they affect your change effort. For example, the attitude *We have always done it this way so I don't want to change* is common. Some people are stubborn and won't budge if left to themselves.

CASE STUDY: HOW INTRODUCING A NEW PROCEDURE WENT TERRIBLY WRONG

A big Australian bank set about introducing a new procedure for assessing their financial risk when lending money. The procedure would impact customers and employees in lots of different ways. It was brought to management's attention early on that employees were not engaged enough to make the change work; they didn't understand how the change was going to make their jobs easier or make lending outcomes better for customers. But the bank's leaders pushed on regardless, believing that it was just anxiety around having to do things differently and it would subside over time. Mostly they ignored it. After six months had passed, the change was entrenched in the bank's policies and resistance to the change was not only persistent but it was growing. More employees were becoming negative about the new way of working, and more problems were noticed by leaders, who found themselves spending far too much time dealing with morale issues than was usual. Months were spent resolving the issues and repairing people's trust in the new practice. All of this angst could have been avoided if the bank's leaders had taken seriously the initial advice that people were starting to reject the change and genuinely set out to do something about it.

EXERCISE 9.1: CREATE AN ENGAGEMENT PLAN

The purpose of this exercise is to define engagement activities that will create energy and excitement in the minds of your employees about what's happening in the business while the change is being implemented.

WHAT TO DO

1. Decide on what you want to engage your team in and list the type of activities you are going to run to achieve that.

2. Complete **Template 9.1: Engagement Plan**. Here is an example of what a completed template looks like. Follow the instructions below on how to complete yours. For a free downloadable version of this template, go to *www.adaptusconsulting.com.au*

Section A	Section B	Section C			Section D	Section E	
Engagement Activity	Description	Audience			Cost	Responsibility	
		Who	When	Where		Organiser	Approver
End of training celebration	Morning tea to celebrate employees' completion of the training and awards for highest achievers	All employees who attended training	Tuesday 18th June, 10am-10.30am	Lunchroom	$75 food + $40 prizes	Steve F	Mary T

3. In **Section A**, name the activity you are going to run. For examples of engagement activities, refer below.

Engagement

Employee engagement is not an exact science but there are endless ideas to promote goodwill.

Here are some ways to gain people's interest and drive engagement in a changing environment:
- Just walk the floor and say *Thanks*, be personal and give some of your time.
- Host a morning tea or lunch to celebrate a milestone.
- Create a newsletter and capture highlights of what's happening across your business.
- Give out certificates of appreciation for examples of extra effort.
- Bring in a speaker to give a motivational presentation.
- Monetary incentives are appropriate in some situations.
- Have a themed workday using decorations or props.
- Create an activity using social media.
- Create a version of the Employee of the Month program to be a meaningful expression of the change you are implementing; e.g. Customer Focus Champion, Quiz Master.
- Create a reward and recognition program to acknowledge the ideas and suggestions your employees make that are put into action.
- As simple as it may seem, socialising with your employees is an easy way to engage with them, whether it be a drink after work or a BBQ on the weekend. Getting together in a non-work environment is very effective at getting teams of people to bond.
- Your workers, above all else, are people. You can create engagement in the workplace by being caring, honest and open. Being responsive in conversation or with requests, and being reliable and consistent in decision and action also create engagement.
- Put the responsibility of implementing the change into the hands of your leaders or supervisors. Give them accountability and allow them to 'own' a part of the change.

- Create a co-worker bonus program by allowing employees to nominate a colleague that went above and beyond to help another employee get work done.
- Ask employees for their thoughts and suggestions on how to execute the change, value their opinions, and then give them ownership of putting their own ideas into action.
- Publicly praise behaviour that models the change so others can see how they should be behaving too.
- Set up *Lunch and Learn* sessions with employees and senior leaders to promote casual conversations about the change.
- Allow employees time to create a video demonstrating what the new way of working means to them or the benefits to their role or team.
- Make candid updates on social media platforms (e.g. Yammer) that employees can make comments on.
- Take photos of employees adopting the change, display them in the lunchroom, and caption it with "Best examples of the [change] in action", or similar.
- Create a newsletter to communicate positive consequences of the change for customers or suppliers, add humour, use cartoons, and get employees involved.
- Run a competition to test people's knowledge of the change.
- Create a *Smart Ideas* program to solicit innovative suggestions from your team and reward the best idea givers.
- Talk about the change with everyone in different ways. Always come back to the Change Goal – the *why* we are doing this and *where* we are going and *what* we will have when we get there.

4. In **Section B**, describe how you will engage your team to adapt to the change.

5. In **Section C**, record:
   a. Who is the activity for?
   b. When will it take place?
   c. Where will the activity take place?

6. In **Section D**, if relevant, record the cost of the activity.

7. In **Section E**, record the details of:
   a. Who is responsible for organising the activity?
   b. Who needs to approve it?

8. Repeat steps 3 – 7 for each engagement activity in your list.

WHAT TO DO NEXT

All the preparation time and effort you're putting into engaging your team in the change will dramatically increase your chances of success. The focus of the next chapter is to create a Feedback Plan to get employees to identify when problems arise before they cause any lasting damage or disruption to your business.

TEMPLATE 9.1: ENGAGEMENT PLAN

Engagement Activity	Description	Audience		When	Where	Cost	Responsibility	
		Who					Organiser	Approver
Name of the activity	Description of what the activity will be about	Who will be involved?		When will it take place?	Where will it take place?	What costs are involved?	Who will organise it?	Who will approve it?

STAGE 2 DEFINE – HOW EMPLOYEES WILL GIVE FEEDBACK

THINK LIKE A WISE MAN BUT COMMUNICATE IN THE LANGUAGE OF THE PEOPLE

WILLIAM YEATS – POET

Feedback is a useful tool to ensure your change is a success. Feedback gives you access to invaluable information and insights that can deepen your understanding of what is happening in your organisation, how employees are feeling from the impact of the change, and solutions to fixing problems.

In this chapter you will create a Feedback Plan. The best plan to have is one that collects feedback at different stages in the change process.

As a guide you might consider:

- What activities have been planned during the change process? What do I want feedback on?
- What do I want to know as my employees progress through their learning activities?
- What questions should I ask to give me insight into how people are feeling about the change?
- Who should I ask?
- When should I ask my employees to tell me how the change is impacting them and if they are feeling supported?
- How will I create a safe place or process for my employees to give honest and open responses?
- How will I collect and analyse the feedback and share the results?
- What questions will I need to ask at the end of the implementation to ensure my employees are engaged with the new mode of operation?
- What might I want to ask them a month after change-over day to ensure things are on track?
- How will I thank people for their feedback and contributions?

Seeking feedback from employees allows new ideas on how to change better, faster, and more effectively to flow through to you. The feedback you receive will help to identify obstacles before they exist. It will tell you if workers are hearing the right messages and how committed they are. It can help you judge who is supporting or resisting the change, and how performance is being affected. Engaging your employees in the process of deciding what feedback to take on and what to ignore will create even more willingness and desire to make the change a success.

CASE STUDY: PUTTING FEEDBACK TO GOOD USE

A bank was rolling out a new computer system for branch tellers to use with customers. During the project, feedback was collected at the beginning to ensure that teller employees were aware of the change. Mid-way through, feedback was obtained to judge how supportive supervisors were with allowing time away from the counter to attend training. Towards the end, near the change-over date, employees were asked for feedback on their level of confidence about switching over to the *new way we do things around here*. Each time feedback was received, improvements to the change-over process, communication and training methods were made which ensured the rollout was successful.

EXERCISE 10.1: CREATE A FEEDBACK PLAN

The purpose of this exercise is to determine *what* feedback you want to gather, *how* and *when*.

WHAT TO DO

1. Make a list of topics or activities you want to evaluate or receive feedback on during the change period.

2. Complete **Template 10.1: Feedback Plan**. Here is an example of what a completed template looks like. Follow the instructions below on how to complete yours. For a free downloadable version of this template, go to ***www. adaptusconsulting.com.au***

Section A	Section B	Section C			Section D	Section E			
		Audience				Responsibility			
Activity	Description	Who	How	When	Cost	Organiser	Reviewer	Decider	Follow-up
Assess effectiveness of Create Maintenance Notification training	Ask 5 questions to rate the effectiveness of the session and what can be improved	OH&S Officers	Printed handout	After they attend training	$25 for materials	John S	Mary T; David P	Mary T	David P

3. In **Section A**, name the activity. For examples of feedback activities, refer below.

Feedback Activity

There are lots of ways you can ask for feedback. The approach you choose needs to suit your culture and the type of change being introduced.

Here are some ideas:
- Have a one-on-one conversation with a range of employees from across your business, at different levels of seniority.
- Run a team workshop. Talk about how the change is going, what's working, and what's not.
- Ask your employees to complete an anonymous survey; this method is great for getting a really honest response to employee engagement and the level of confidence people have with the new solution.
- Observe the change in action. Arrange someone to watch over an area of your business where the change has been introduced, and make observations about how well the change has been implemented. Get them to use a checklist, tally up the score and compare it to other areas of the business.
- Evaluate output by measuring productivity before, during and after the change for comparison.
- Arrange an interactive session where every participant receives live feedback from the group about their contribution to the

change, and every person gives feedback to others, including you. Questions such as *What are you doing to implement the change?* and *What holds you back from embracing the change?* can be useful in this context.

- Track fluctuations in performance. A dip in productivity in a particular area of your business could indicate resistance, or a low willingness to take on the new approach to working.
- Interview your clients. Ask them questions that will help you discover if they're seeing or experiencing the positive impacts of the change.
- Measure error rates or calls to your help desk by reviewing the number of problems, issues, complaints or defects. Watch for variation; it may indicate an obstacle has arisen.
- Assess usage statistics. Check the numbers of logins, uploads, downloads, or time spent using a system before and after the change; the answers could indicate a skill deficiency.
- Alternatively, you could just interact informally with your employees and show an interest in what they are doing to adapt to the change. Ask questions about their approach to embedding the change in their working day, and listen.

4. In **Section B**, describe the activity and questions you will ask. For sample questions, refer below.

Questions

Here are examples of feedback questions you might ask in conversation, a workshop or a team meeting:
- Describe what's working well for us so far and what's not.
- What ideas do you have to change that?
- How can we do things differently to make the change happen faster or better?
- How much time have you had to learn and practice the new skills? Has it been enough?
- What support have you received? Do you need more?
- How is your supervisor helping you to understand how the change is affecting your team/department?

- Are any problems starting to emerge? What do you think is the cause?
- What ideas do you have to solve those problems?
- How good has the communication been so far?
- What would you like to know more of?
- How do you feel about the change?
- What are you worried about?
- What's easy? What's hard?
- Have your team's performance levels been affected? Better or worse?
- What impact has the change had on production levels?
- If there's a problem, what can we do to fix it?
- Have you noticed any new obstacles starting to arise?
- How would you like to celebrate our achievements?

5. In **Section C**, record:
   a. Who will participate in providing feedback?
   b. How will the feedback activity be conducted?
   c. When will employees participate?

6. In **Section D**, if relevant, record the cost of obtaining the feedback.

7. In **Section E**, record details of:
   a. Who is responsible for running the activity?
   b. Who will review the feedback?
   c. Who will decide on what is to be actioned?
   d. Who will present the findings and communicate to the rest of your workforce which actions will be taken up? For an understanding of the importance of follow-up, refer below.

Follow-up

There is an important matter to be emphasised: if you are not committed to acting on the feedback you receive, don't ask for it. When employees give feedback openly but see no result or action, morale takes a hit and trust is damaged. It's worse than not asking for any feedback at all. At least if no one has been asked for feedback, there is no expectation of an explanation or mitigation.

On the other hand, it is OK *not* to act on feedback, but what is vital in this situation is to explain *why*. Be open and transparent and authentic. If the reason is cost, viability, relevance, or something else, say so. That way your employees will know they have been heard and engagement levels won't be harmed.

Letting your people know what you intend on doing with the feedback needs to be built into your plan too.

8. Now repeat steps 3 – 7 for each feedback activity in your list.

WHAT TO DO NEXT

You are nearing the end of the Define stage and will appreciate that there is a lot to do to manage change well. Seeking help is important. It's unlikely that you will be able to undertake every planned activity without help which is why the focus of the next chapter is to create a Support Plan.

TEMPLATE 10.1: FEEDBACK PLAN

| Activity | Description | Audience | | | Cost | Responsibility | | | |
		Who	How	When		Organiser	Reviewer	Decider	Follow-up
Name of the activity	Description of the activity or questions to be asked	Who will participate?	How will they participate?	When will they participate?	What costs are involved?	Who will organise it?	Who will review the responses?	Who will decide on the action to take?	Who will communicate the outcome with employees?

STAGE 2 DEFINE – HOW EMPLOYEES WILL ASSIST THE CHANGE EFFORT

LEADERSHIP IS THE ART OF GETTING SOMEONE ELSE TO DO SOMETHING YOU WANT DONE BECAUSE HE WANTS TO DO IT

DWIGHT D EISENHOWER - FORMER PRESIDENT

Saying, doing, and acting on all the right things to make a change successful can be exhausting if you're the only person responsible. Imagine trying to champion the Change Goal, organise the training, communicate the updates, answer questions, deal with resistance, collect feedback and arrange milestone celebrations by yourself. That would be very hard work, and you have a business to run. So you need to share the responsibilities and delegate. To do that you need to recruit Change Supporters. Change Supporters foster engagement. A Change Supporter is someone who believes in the change, who will actively promote it to others, and will help you action your change plans. It's a good idea to ask for volunteers; tapping into highly motivated people who want to see the change succeed is a great way to solicit Change Support.

In this chapter you will create a Support Plan. The more people you empower to help manage the change, the more engagement you will build, the more invested they will feel in the outcome, and the greater your chances of success.

EXERCISE 11.1: CREATE A SUPPORT PLAN

The purpose of this exercise is to define the tasks you want your Change Supporters to carry out for you.

WHAT TO DO

1. Make a list of tasks you want your employees to help you with during the change period.

2. Identify employees who are willing to become Change Supporters. It also helps if they are well known, have credibility in your company, and if you trust them to help you manage the change. For help with choosing Change Supporters, refer below.

Choosing Change Supporters

Choose people who listen, are considerate in their thinking, are respected and valued in the workplace and who have something worthwhile to say when they speak.

A word of caution: don't choose people who big-note themselves, don't listen, share, or respect the opinions of others. People who only like the sound of their own voice and cannot listen to others cause frustration. People who undermine others' opinions are undermining teamwork, and ultimately jeopardise the goodwill that forms when a group of people band together for a common cause.

3. Complete **Template 11.1: Support Plan**. Here is an example of what a completed template looks like. Follow the instructions below on how to complete yours. For a free downloadable version of this template, go to **www.adaptusconsulting.com.au**

Section A	Section B	Section C	Section D	Section E		
				Audience		
Support Task	Description	Responsibility	Cost	Who	How	When
Post-training follow up	Follow up with each team after they've received training to check how confident they feel with the new process	John S	$0	All teams	Attend weekly team meeting & discuss	30th July

4. In **Section A**, record the task you want the Change Supporters to undertake. For examples of typical tasks you may require support with, refer below.

Support Tasks

Tasks you might ask Change Supporters to do could include:

Communication – Writing and managing the communications to employees. Being available to answer employees' questions.

Training – Determining when, where and how the training or learning will be done, as well as when and how employees will practise. How will performance be measured?

Support – Following up with employees back on-the-job to make sure they feel reassured. Monitoring productivity fluctuations, or quality of forms, or impacts to timelines – whatever needs to be monitored.

Issues – Deal with people issues, performance issues, communication issues, support issues, etc.

Feedback – Collecting feedback and reporting it back to management or the business owner.

Celebrations – Arranging the celebrations, selecting rewards, creating award certificates, etc.

---

5. In **Section B**, describe the task.

6. In **Section C**, record the name of the employee who has been nominated or volunteered.

7. In **Section D**, if relevant, record the cost of the task.

8. In **Section E**, record:
   a. Which employees will be affected by the task?
   b. How will the task be conducted?
   c. When will the task be actioned?

9. Now repeat steps 4 – 8 for each task in your list.

WHAT TO DO NEXT

Well done! You are at the end of the Define stage. The next chapter focuses on applying your Learning, Communication, and Engagement Plans to support your employees while they adopt new skills and support the transition of your business through the change.

SUMMARY OF STAGE 2: DEFINE

- New ways of working need to be taught. To know what people need to learn, you need to discover how your business will be *impacted* by the change.
- When it comes to change in the workplace, there is no such thing as too much communication. Good communication is simple, clear, and delivered in multiple ways.
- Building employee engagement during the change process results in fewer people becoming discouraged when something goes wrong or becomes hard.
- Business leaders who are considered trustworthy and fair establish credibility with two-way communication and by allowing employees to give feedback.

- Getting feedback during the change process helps to identify obstacles before they exist, gives insight into resistant behaviour, and indicates how performance is being affected.
- Change Supporters help to share the responsibility of leading the change and contribute to building engagement.
- Creating Learning, Communications, Engagement, Feedback and Support Plans sets a changing business up for success by minimising things *not going according to plan.*

TEMPLATE 11.1: SUPPORT PLAN

Support Task	Description	Responsibility	Cost	Audience			When
				Who	How		When
Name of the support task	What will the Change Supporter need to do?	Who is the Change Supporter?	What costs are involved?	Who will the task affect?	How will the task be undertaken?		When will it happen?

STAGE 3 APPLY – YOUR CHANGE PLANS AND ACTIVITIES

WILLINGNESS TO CHANGE IS A STRENGTH, EVEN IF IT MEANS PLUNGING PART OF THE COMPANY INTO TOTAL CONFUSION FOR A WHILE

JACK WELCH – FORMER CEO, GENERAL ELECTRIC

In the previous stage of the *Adapt Method*, you created a set of plans for how you will manage the change in your business. You can now move your organisation into the new *business as usual* state swiftly by applying those plans.

In this chapter you will:
• apply your Learning Plan
• ramp up communications and employee engagement to build an atmosphere of trust, openness and sharing
• apply your Support Plan.

By completing the Learning Plan exercise earlier, you created a bridge to manage the gap between how employees currently do their jobs and the *new* skills and knowledge they need … knowledge such as what employees need to be trained on, how the instruction will be provided, what on-the-job practice and coaching is needed, and the tools required to support the learning. All Learning, Communications, and Engagement effort at this time should be focused on helping your employees to grasp the new skills they need to make the change successfully.

EXERCISE 12.1: APPLY THE LEARNING PLAN

The purpose of this exercise is to carry out your Learning Plan.

WHAT TO DO

1. Carry out the learning activities captured in your Plan. Different people have different learning capabilities. Be mindful of the differences in each of your employees' capacity to learn. Not everybody will have the same ability to develop new skills.

2. Ensure employees can practise their new skills. For information on the importance of practice to enable learning, refer below.

Practice makes perfect

If you are expecting employees to change the working habits they've built up over many years with a short training course, you will be disappointed. Whilst dedicated learning experiences away from the job are useful ways to prepare employees for change, it rarely results in performance change being sustained long term.

Training often doesn't address the social skills and attitudes needed back on the job. Retention problems arise if there is a time-gap between learning something new in a training session and being able to apply it; people forget what they have learned if they can't immediately use it.

In addition, personal issues of resistance, fear of change, and complacency can all reduce the effects of training events. It's not until employees are required to practise in their normal day-to-day working environment that true skills transfer can take effect.

A valuable principle in adult learning is nicely expressed by this Chinese proverb: Tell me and I'll forget; show me and I may remember; involve me and I'll understand. This means that although attendance at formal training programs is useful to learning new skills, on-the-job practice is vital to sustain that new learning.

Practice and supportive coaching in the context of a person's day job will allow:
- problems they encounter to be addressed without consequence
- gaps in understanding or skill to be taken care of
- undesirable attitudes to be identified and dealt with
- the change to be introduced in a much less threatening way
- fear of the unknown to be dealt with kindly
- opportunity to fail, learn from mistakes, and real behaviour changes to set in.

If opportunities to practice are given they must be directly linked to a person's role and be undertaken in a real-world context. Imagine if the only option given to you to learn how to drive a car was by reading a book. How competent a driver would you be? Suffice to say you cannot learn how to drive without being able to practise in a real car on a real road. It is the same for your workforce when they're trying to master new skills. Employees need to have the opportunity to practise, make mistakes, learn, and try again. Practice makes perfect – it's true!

Don't miss this step; eventually your business will be affected in one-way or another. The time used for practice will far and away be less than the time needed to address live issues of poor performance when it really counts.

WHAT TO DO NEXT

By now employees will see that the change has begun to take effect. Communication is an important tool for keeping employees involved and actively participating in the change. People act on their emotions and are inspired by compelling ideas. Initiating stimulating conversations that tap into the emotional benefits of the Change Goal will engage your employees. The Communications Plan exercise helped you to define what employees need to hear about what's changing. The next exercise will bring that plan to life.

EXERCISE 12.2: RAMP UP COMMUNICATION

The purpose of this exercise is to carry out your Communications Plan.

WHAT TO DO

1. Carry out the communication activities captured in your Plan. For information on timing, relevance and how to manage good communication, refer below.

When Enough Isn't Enough

Even when communication is constant, some people still complain that it isn't enough. This reaction doesn't mean you should create more communications, have more meetings, or issue more newsletters or more email. What they are really saying usually stems from one of the following problems.

Problem	Techniques to overcome the problem
The communication process isn't two-way	One-way communication all the time is like one hand clapping: fruitless. So remember, when talking with your workforce, create an

equal number of opportunities to allow two-way conversations so employees feel there's a chance to ask questions, give their opinions and be heard.

The timing of the communication is too late or too early	If your messages aren't timed right they will lack context. People will be missing background information and won't be able to create a full picture in their minds.
The relevance of the information is poor	If you send the right message to the wrong people it will cause confusion. Understanding that different employees in your business need different communications, and then segmenting your messages accordingly will ensure they are relevant.
There are barriers to getting the information they *really* need	If you're not giving employees the information they really want then no amount of saying the same thing over and over is going to satisfy them. It seems obvious but you need to ask them what they want to know and when, then deliver it to them.

2. Enhance the listening appeal of your spoken and written communications. For information on improving the listening appeal of your message, refer below.

Listening appeal

Listening appeal is a characteristic of speaking that catches people's attention so that they retain more of the message. Making the concepts relate to your employees' situation, and the personal benefits to them, is a good place to start. If you can make your communication clear and enhance your listening appeal, you increase the likelihood that employees will listen to what you have to say.

Listening appeal is enhanced when these principles are followed:

- **Clear** – You know exactly what it is you have to tell people and organise the words in your mind in a clear and simple manner.
- **Action** – You know exactly what it is you want them to do.
- **Concise** – You are able to articulate your message without waffle.
- **Language** – You use language and phrases that your employees can understand and relate to; avoid jargon.
- **Tone** – You use a tone that is positive and encouraging.
- **Context** – Draw on your Change Goal and relate the message back to that to give people a sense of the bigger picture.

WHAT TO DO NEXT

When elements of trust, openness and sharing are present, interactions between employees and management are more authentic, and politics and self-interest are minimised. Most people genuinely want to do a good job and be part of a winning team. With support and encouragement, your employees will go a long way to be part of *your* winning team.

Previously you defined engagement activities that will generate energy and enthusiasm about the change within your workforce. In this exercise you will ramp-up your employee engagement focus. Highly engaged, empowered employees will contribute far more to improving your organisation and its performance than any other lever you might pull. The next exercise will deepen the engagement levels between your employees and the change.

EXERCISE 12.3: ACT ON THE ENGAGEMENT PLAN

The purpose of this exercise is to carry out your Engagement Plan.

WHAT TO DO

1. Carry out the Engagement activities captured in your plan.
    For tips on how to build engagement, refer below.

Engagement tips

Here are some tips to help you engage employees:

*   **Gratitude furthers engagement** – Recognising an individual's initiative or contribution towards the change process is a powerful motivator for engagement. It doesn't take much time or effort to recognise or reward employees who are willingly giving extra effort or thought to the achievement of the Change Goal.

*   **Encourage initiative and innovation** – If employees are allowed the leeway to make small improvements to their work, it's likely that your business will become a little bit better, or faster, or safer, or cost-efficient. Now imagine if you used this approach while your business is in transition. The effect would improve engagement and foster innovation. Shifting focus from purely production to production and improvement will increase enthusiasm and effort, and enable you to further the Change Goal. People get a lot of satisfaction out of the freedom to implement their own ideas. And it all leads to the same place: creating a highly engaged environment.

*   **Implement your employees' good ideas** – Employees are motivated when they see something valuable happening with their ideas. Seeking input about problems and solutions from your team will generate engagement.

*   **Manage poor attitude** – You will need to manage fluctuations in motivation and mood during a transition, and help employees get past stumbling blocks. If left to fester, the poor attitude of one team member can infect the attitudes of others. You need to deal with it swiftly but with kindness and empathy. Openly discuss why they feel the way they do. Coach them on the benefits of moving to a new way of operating. Be firm, too, about the consequences of continuing to be negative and not getting on board.

- **Give support generously** – In the end, getting people on board is about encouraging them, allowing them some control of their daily work processes, giving them room to make little improvements, providing an environment to offer up feedback, and support to learn and grow at the same pace your business does.

2. Observe your business to judge the level of employee engagement you can see. Eliminate behaviour that undermines the engagement you are trying to build. For information on what can damage engagement, refer below.

Mistakes to Avoid

It is normal for employees to feel uncertain about change, lack confidence in their abilities to change, or find ways to resist. Leaders who cannot or won't provide help and support to employees during times of change make it more difficult for people to cope. Here are some leadership behaviours that damage engagement. Avoid making these common mistakes when your business is trying to transition to a new state.

Common Behaviour	Common Consequence
Responding negatively to mistakes made while learning	Leaders who embarrass or reject employees who make mistakes or who speak up about difficult situations destroy engagement. Employees must see that they are respected. Positive, supportive relationships between employees and leaders are crucial to your business changing successfully.
Not recognising that we all view the world differently	This can lead to relationship conflicts. When people struggle to make a connection or can't work well together, it's often because they see the work at hand from a different perspective. Use the Change Goal to rally your employees and respectfully acknowledge their opinions while holding firm to the reasons why the business must change.

Being too controlling	People need to work in a reasonably stable and predictable environment, but they don't want to *be* controlled. They want freedom to succeed, but with limits and responsibilities. People are more likely to resist force than they are to resist change and uncertainty. Asserting full control over an employee's performance usually puts it into cruise control. That doesn't mean everyone in your organisation should be involved in every decision, but employees should have a say in *some* decisions, especially the ones that affect them.
Treating people as unintelligent	People, unlike animals, have the unique capacity to use imagination to create things and innovate. People also have the unique capacity of free will: the ability to make their own choices. In a work environment, if you don't allow people the opportunity to use their initiative, you not only restrict their free will, but you eventually kill their imagination. This wastes the opportunity for innovation to blossom, or improvement ideas to be offered, or for anything to be leaner, smarter, faster, or better. Treat people like they don't have intelligence and they will leave their brains at the door in the morning and pick them up on the way out at night.

3. Check-in with leaders and employees to identify any instances of resistance and deal with it. For information on dealing with resistance, refer below.

Responding to Resistance

Resistance can present itself at any stage of the change journey – beginning, middle, end, and even after the change becomes business as usual. Typically, resistance will be at its highest in the Apply stage.

Employees often oppose change if they fear it will have a detrimental effect on their security, personal finances, working relationships, level of responsibility, or if they are not trained and supported properly. As the pace of change increases in your business, it is likely that anxiety levels will rise. Within this atmosphere you will have some active supporters, some resistors, and some people just waiting to see what happens. Sometimes it's a whole team of people resisting a change. At other times it's a supervisor, with their influence and authority, who is quietly being defiant. Either way, you need to identify it and resolve it, or it will smoulder and possibly weaken the commitment and energy of other teams nearby.

For detailed guidance on how to manage resistance, refer to *Chapter 15: Dealing with Resistance.*

Managing day-to-day operations, while at the same time trying to alter the way you operate, may feel like hard work unless your employees assist. A good way to alleviate the extra pressure of introducing change into your business is to use trusted employees to assist … which is the focus of the next exercise.

EXERCISE 12.4: APPLY THE SUPPORT PLAN

The purpose of this exercise is to prepare your chosen employees to take on the role of Change Supporter and guide you to carry out your Support Plan.

WHAT TO DO

1. Arrange a meeting and invite your Change Supporters to attend.

2. Check that the group is still connected to the Change Goal and feels change-ready. This part of the process is important as it gets any misunderstandings out into the open early, avoiding problems later.

3. Discuss the tasks you want them to do. Ask for volunteers for each task. That way, people put their hand up for things they are interested in and care about.

4. Discuss issue resolution and gain agreement on how these factors should be handled.

5. Agree on the chain of command for making decisions and communicating outcomes. Change Supporters need to know which issues can be dealt with immediately with no consultation, and which can't. Be clear about what decision-making authority your supporters have and when they need to consult you.

6. Discuss how regularly you will catch up with your Change Supporters, and agree on the meeting agenda. Change Support meetings are a good environment to deal with rumours, misinformation and resistance issues. Set this expectation up from the start, make it a standing agenda item, and ask for disclosure every meeting.

7. Instruct your Change Supporters to carry out the activities in the Support Plan.

8. Set up future meetings on a regular basis.

9. Use future meetings to get feedback from the Change Supporters on how employees are feeling about being impacted by the change.

10. Encourage open and transparent dialogue. Urge them to talk regularly to their colleagues about the Change Goal, benefits, impacts and issues. Have them connect the change to the reality at the local level.

11. Recognise their participation in what is a very important undertaking for your business.

WHAT TO DO NEXT

Well done. You are at the end of the Apply stage. The next chapter focuses on preventing issues and obstacles derailing your change project.

SUMMARY

- Providing meaningful learning activities and ensuring employees practise their new skills back on the job will help to sustain a change in behaviour.
- If you communicate clearly and enhance your listening appeal, employees will both listen and understand what you have to say.
- Balancing freedom and control among employees allows imagination to flourish.
- Giving praise generously builds good will.
- Including employees in the decision-making that impacts them creates motivation to adapt to change.

STAGE 4 PREVENT – ISSUES DERAILING THE CHANGE EFFORT

THE FIRST RESISTANCE TO CHANGE IS TO SAY IT'S NOT NECESSARY

GLORIA STEINEM – ACTIVIST

The most important targets to hit to manage change well are: teach new skills effectively, allow your employees to practise to gain confidence, communicate often, and engage them in where you are trying to take your business. Yet even if you do all this well, employees generally won't get on board if they feel disempowered because obstacles exist in your business that prevent them from implementing the change. Preventing obstacles from derailing the change effort and asking for feedback to improve the change process is the focus of this chapter.

In this chapter you will learn how to:

- identify internal business structures or systems that conflict with the change
- manage people-blockers
- action your Feedback Plan to prevent unknown problems from emerging by asking employees for improvement ideas to refine the change process.

Imagine you're introducing a new sales approach. Substantial time and effort has been invested into developing the knowledge, skills and attitude of your sales team. But you've overlooked one important obstacle: the old appraisal system. Your sales employees are currently judged on time management, number of prospects and short-term sales volume. But the new approach expects them to focus on developing a deeper, broader client relationship to generate long-term sales volumes. This puts the appraisal system in conflict with the Change Goal and it will hamper success. To make a successful change in your business you need to ensure your organisational design supports the Change Goal. This is the focus of the next exercise.

EXERCISE 13.1: PREVENT OR ELIMINATE OBSTRUCTIONS

The purpose of this exercise is to deal with people and organisational obstructions in your business that can slow down or stop the change being a success.

WHAT TO DO

1. Examine your business systems and look for conflicts between your organisational design and the Change Goal.

Common Organisational Conflicts

If the issue of incompatibility between the change and existing systems is not addressed, chances are people's behaviour will revert back to the old ways of doing things. All systems need to be in harmony with the *new ways* for the change to succeed. Involving your employees to seek out systems that are in conflict, and creating ways to align them, is both supportive of engagement *and* proactive in addressing potential resistance.

Conflict can arise:
- if reward systems are misaligned to the change. For example, people are expected to change how they work, but the reward or bonus system that is attached to that behaviour is not updated to match the new expectations. This type of conflict is highly demotivating in any business context. It's easily fixed but many businesses undergoing change don't think to do it
- if praise is inappropriately given. For example, active teamwork and collaboration is expected but only the best performing individuals are recognised, or innovation is encouraged but only technical proficiency in old, existing technologies is recognised
- if job descriptions limit employees being innovative or productive after the change
- if new recruits are not assessed for alignment with the Change Goal
- if performance appraisal systems don't motivate employees to display the new behaviours
- if Key Performance Indicators (KPIs) are not created to mandate the new way of working
- if promotional activity is at odds with the new way of operating
- if hierarchy, management structures, or siloes exist that don't complement the new way the business wants to operate
- if resources or support is inadequate to meet the Change Goal
- if strategic direction is out-of-sync with the Change Goal.

2. Identify leaders who use a command-and-control style of leadership and address this behaviour. Command-and-

control styles of leadership disempower people to the point where if it is not addressed, it can destabilise a whole change effort.

3. Identify people or behaviours not aligning to the Change Goal and manage this resistance. For information on managing people-blockers, refer below.

Managing People-Blockers

Ideally, you want all employees, especially leaders, to be aligned with the business's direction at all times. When a change comes about and someone doesn't or can't re-align themselves, then tension is created. Tension in that individual. Tension in the team. Tension in the business. The tension the individual feels is self-inflicted, but nevertheless it is real and can have a flow-on effect to other employees.

To address this situation you can:
- take action through honest dialogue that targets the undesirable behaviour head on
- redeploy blockers to another team, department or role
- exit blockers out of your business
- it might sound harsh, but if blockers cannot align with the goals of your business, it's in their best interest, and yours, to ease them out with respect and dignity. This notion may seem to fly in the face of engagement but removing obstructions, especially in your leadership hierarchy, will have the effect of empowering others to act.

For more information, refer to *Chapter 15: Dealing with Resistance*.

4. Resolve the issues you have identified so that your business systems are in harmony with the Change Goal.

WHAT TO DO NEXT

Although not fool proof, the exercise you have completed will usually flush out the major obstacles that may exist in your business. The rest can be identified through employee feedback, which is the focus of the next exercise.

USING FEEDBACK TO IDENTIFY PROBLEMS AND OBSTRUCTIONS

Seeking feedback is important because if you aren't impacting your workforce in the right way, the change won't stick, your employees won't adopt it fully, and over time the benefits you expect won't be sustained.

Gathering feedback will help you discover:
- what people are thinking and feeling about the change
- what's working and what's not
- what messages are getting through
- how onboard your employees are
- if performance or production is being affected positively or negatively
- if new problems are starting to arise.

No one person has a monopoly on good ideas. That's why collecting feedback will help you make adjustments and improve your approach. And it often identifies problems before they become a headache.

CASE STUDY: FEEDBACK SUPPORTS BUSINESS CHANGE

A company used social media to engage their employees in an online, real-time conversation about how to improve their internal practices as part of a new program of work. Employees were encouraged to contribute their ideas and make constructive criticisms. People indicated support of the good ideas by 'liking' them. Owners of those popular ideas were empowered to set up a team and make the changes happen. Not only did it energise the company's workforce by creating a widespread, open conversation, but it improved morale by setting people up to contribute worthwhile ideas and successfully improved the *way we do things around here.*

EXERCISE 13.2: ACTION THE FEEDBACK PLAN

The purpose of this exercise is to carry out your Feedback Plan.

WHAT TO DO

1. Carry out the feedback activities captured in your plan. For information on which method to use for different types of feedback, refer below.

Choosing Feedback Methods

The Methods table below provides guidelines for gathering feedback and taking action.

Approach	Suitable collection methods						Action
	One-on-one conversation	Workshop, focus group or meeting	Survey	Observation	Usage Statistics	Interview	
To know what people are thinking and feeling, ask trusted or well-respected people from across your business, in different roles, and at different levels of seniority.	✔	✔	✔			✔	Identify areas of concern. Share these insights and gather ideas you think will address the problems or obstacles. Ask impacted teams to action the solutions in their area.
To gauge overall levels of engagement, you need to encourage discussions about how the change is working and what's not.	✔	✔	✔			✔	
To check communication is effective, ask for people's opinion and satisfaction with what they have been told. Is it enough? Too much? Relevant? Timely?	✔	✔	✔			✔	Share the feedback and ideas given. State clearly how you will address the problems raised. Empower employees who initiated the idea to implement the solutions.

Approach	Suitable collection methods						Action
	One-on-one conversation	Workshop, focus group or meeting	Survey	Observation	Usage Statistics	Interview	
To assess if learning activities are adequate and effective look at how much time supervisors are spending helping or overseeing activity. Ask if employees are sufficiently competent in the new skills. Check if time spent completing tasks or error rates is more than expected. Look for variations in productivity levels before and after the change, or between employees in the same role. This can indicate inconsistent skill development or the need for more training.	✔			✔	✔		Review the Learning Plan. Consider providing more on-the-job tools to help people. Has there been enough practice time allowed? Do employees understand how the process or tasks have altered? If learning was only offered using one method (e.g.: classroom style), consider offering coaching or allow individuals to observe someone role-modeling the new way of working.

Approach	Suitable collection methods						Action
	One-on-one conversation	Workshop, focus group or meeting	Survey	Observation	Usage Statistics	Interview	
To gauge confidence in the solution, ask questions to discover if employees still believe the business is delivering the change successfully and feel confident the benefits can be realised.	✔	✔	✔			✔	Review the solution and address the concerns raised or communicate how the solution overcomes the issues. Provide more information or demonstrate the solution if employees haven't seen it working yet.
To identify resistance or employees who are not on board with the change, identify who is resisting. Use empathy to understand why. Is it because they can't change? Don't want to change? Don't understand how, or why? Aren't getting enough support, or time to change? Don't have enough direction, or are struggling with how to let go of the old ways of doing things?	✔	✔	✔	✔	✔	✔	Refer to *Chapter 15 Dealing with Resistance*. People who are resisting the change are not engaged – get them back on board.

Approach	Suitable collection methods						Action
	One-on-one conversation	Workshop, focus group or meeting	Survey	Observation	Usage Statistics	Interview	
To track fluctuations in performance, identify errors, problems, issues, complaints or failures, collect data and analyse trends, fluctuations, spikes, deviations and anomalies. Alternatively, observe whether tasks are being completed correctly. Use a checklist, score the standard of operation, and compare workers, teams, or lines of business. Check usage numbers, or time spent completing a task. Watch for variation.				✔	✔		Identify the source of the problem – is it a lack of skill, knowledge, communication, engagement or support? A dip in productivity could indicate resistance to change or a lack of guidance or support. Fluctuations could indicate a skill or knowledge deficiency. Changes to error rates may indicate an obstacle has arisen or more education or direction or guidance is required for employees to adopt the change.

Approach	Suitable collection methods						Action
	One-on-one conversation	Workshop, focus group or meeting	Survey	Observation	Usage Statistics	Interview	
To observe the change in action or to determine if the Change Goal is being achieved, watch what people are doing, ask questions, and listen.				✔			Increase the communication and engagement activity. Are employees inspired to change? Are they excited about the future and the benefits? Do they know what's in it for them? Do they care?

2. Spend time listening. For information on the importance of listening when collecting feedback, refer below.

Listening Tool

Listening is an effective tool for learning how well or poorly your business is handling change. Encouraging your workforce to voice their ideas, opinions and give feedback creates enthusiasm and ownership of the change. When people are telling you how it really is for them, sit back, get comfortable, and just listen for a while. If they feel safe to express themselves and you show a genuine desire to hear them out, you'll be amazed at what gems they'll come up with. Experience shows that employees that are involved in discussing the change are more passionate, committed to success, and are greater supporters of what the business is trying to achieve.

---

3. Collate the feedback.

4. Share the findings with your team.

5. If appropriate, invite your team to help decide what feedback to action.

6. Decide together what urgently needs to be fixed, what needs to be fixed at some point, and what's not necessary to fix.

7. Prioritise the issues to be addressed.

8. Ask for volunteers to take responsibility for actioning the feedback.

9. Show appreciation for people's value towards, and participation in, the feedback process by celebrating.

WHAT TO DO NEXT

Well done. You are at the end of the Prevent stage. The next chapter focuses on transferring the change into your business culture and making sure it sticks.

SUMMARY

- Existing systems need to be in harmony with the change for it to succeed.
- Employees who are encouraged to contribute their ideas and provide feedback about the change are more passionate,

committed to its success, and are greater supporters of what the business is trying to achieve.

• Command-and-control styles of leadership must be identified and eradicated to protect the success of a change effort.

CHAPTER 14

STAGE 5 TRANSFER – THE CHANGE INTO BUSINESS-AS-USUAL

IF YOU DO NOT CHANGE DIRECTION, YOU MAY END UP WHERE YOU WERE HEADING

LAO TZU – PHILOSOPHER

A frequent misunderstanding is that all culture change happens at the beginning of a change journey. This is not always true. Sometimes it doesn't set in until well after the change has been transferred into the business, is showing positive, predictable results, and is being reinforced.

A business change is considered adopted when a workforce displays the new behaviours, thinking and attitudes *consistently* over an extended period of time. Business owners often think that once the Change Goal has been achieved, the new practices will stick indefinitely. Unfortunately, that isn't always the case. If the new way of working is not properly maintained, or fully anchored into the workplace culture, employees can revert back to the old, less productive behaviours. Evidence suggests that the older your business is, the longer it will take your culture to adopt change.

In this chapter you will:
- reinforce the transference of change into your employees' behaviour
- anchor the change into your business culture with the help of your Change Supporters
- celebrate the achievement of the Change Goal in a way that works for your team
- learn how to gauge whether your change is sticking, and what to do if it isn't.

No one wants an investment in their business disappearing. And everyone wants to see a positive impact to the bottom line. So how do you make sure the change you've made to your business sticks? How can you avoid your workforce reverting back to the old way of doing things? How do you avoid having to put in extra effort to re-engage people again? This stage of the *Adapt Method* provides ways to ensure you get both – *stickiness* and results.

CASE STUDY: MAKING CHANGE STICK IS NOT AUTOMATIC

A glass production company introduced computer automation into what had been a manual manufacturing process. Throughout the change-over period, the *Change Supporters* responsible for implementing the Change Goal did a good job teaching employees how to use the new computer system and letting them know when, why and how things were changing. It was all going well until the support stopped. Soon after support was withdrawn, computer system error rates climbed, employees started to complain that the system was no good, and productivity levels fell.

So what went wrong?

Even though employees had acquired the right skills to operate the new system, the company's management made the mistake of ceasing to support employees back on-the-job where they were still getting comfortable with using the new computer system. They also stopped talking about the benefits to the company of computerisation, and listening to what employees were telling them about day-to-day challenges. In addition, they stopped discussing the transition to automation as the strategic approach to future efforts for creating efficiency and reducing waste. The benefits of a very expensive conversion began to erode as process efficiencies diminished.

If you don't keep lines of communication open to hearing what isn't working well, or you remove support, don't track performance trends, fail to reward adoption, or don't link the change to future business goals, your chance of sustaining a business change is limited. The focus of the next exercise is to safeguard your business from this effect.

EXERCISE 14.1: REINFORCE THE NEW BEHAVIOURS

The purpose of this exercise is to reinforce the change within the minds of your employees.

WHAT TO DO

1. Ask your leaders to actively demonstrate the change. To get the new mode of operation to take root in your culture you need to make it very clear that the new practices *work* and the old habits *don't*. Actively demonstrating the change in a way that's visible to every member of your team will reinforce that the outcome of the change is here to stay.

2. Discuss the change in business planning.
    Discuss how to use the change to target new markets or new customers, or how it can be used to diversify or expand operations. This dialogue will help to confirm in people's minds that the change is here to stay – that there's no going back.

3. Share positive results generously.
    Openly share the positive results created by the change – a rise in sales, a decrease in complaints, higher quality outcomes, greater efficiencies, rise in performance, more collaboration, etc. This will reinforce the benefits of the new work practices.

4. Keep lines of communication open.

   Even when the change has transitioned into business-as-usual, you need to keep the lines of communication open. Allowing people to continue to provide feedback, ask questions, challenge what's not working well, and share what is working, will help the *new way we do things around here* to stick.

5. Recognise employees who have adopted the change well. For information on the importance of reward and recognition, refer below.

Reward and recognition

Reward and recognition has a strong effect on people's willingness to sustain change.

Here are some tips you can use:
- When implementing change, it's wise to exaggerate your demonstration of appreciation and make it highly visible to others. This helps people to know what high performance looks like and what is expected of them.
- Recognition can be as simple as supervisors acknowledging effort in informal, private conversation.
- Publicly recognising an individual is a useful way to create a role model and set the standard for the new behaviour.
- Group celebration is another approach to rewarding high performing change adopters.
- Capturing the new behaviour in people's performance evaluations and appraisals and including it in their productivity goals provides an incentive to maintain the new ways of working.
- People quickly recognise the value of change when it is linked to their pay packet or when given a gift, like a hamper or voucher, which recognises their contribution and effort.
- Creating achievable performance targets is important too as it sends a message that it's possible to obtain recognition.
- Creating new incentives to reward employees who

demonstrate high adoption is effective in sustaining the new operating model. Whatever approach you use, be sure to reward change. It is a proven method to ensure the transfer of new skills and behaviour is sustained.

6. Continue to provide on-the-job support.

    If during the Define Stage you set up on-the-job support, then keep it going after the change effort has ceased. This can take the form of your Supporters retaining responsibility for being the central point of contact for ongoing questions and assistance, or assigning support responsibility to employees in each line of business who have become expert in the new ways of working.

WHAT TO DO NEXT

While you are reinforcing the change in the minds of your employees, you need to simultaneously be reinforcing the change within the culture and operations of your business. The next exercise focuses on strengthening the adoption of the change into your business culture and business-as-usual activities.

EXERCISE 14.2: ANCHOR THE CHANGE INTO BUSINESS-AS-USUAL

The purpose of this exercise is to embed the change into your business-operating model.

Note: Depending on the scale of the change you are managing and the number of employees in your workforce, you may not need to undertake all of the steps in this exercise.

WHAT TO DO

1. Track performance and productivity.
   A clear indication that a change to your business is being maintained is through data. You may have experienced a slight decline in performance during the change-over period whilst your workforce was adapting. However, at some point the benefits of the change will need to present themselves in your business data.

   By collecting data you can monitor and track fluctuations. A drop in productivity may be a symptom of people reverting back to the old, less effective way of working. Or it may indicate a system conflict or a new issue of resistance. In any event, tracking performance and productivity data will allow you to identify issues swiftly should they arise.

2. Share performance and productivity measures.
   Share performance reports and productivity statistics with your employees to reassure them that the change has taken effect and has improved the outlook of the business.

3. Link the change to future business objectives.
   Directly linking current and future business objectives to the new operating model will reinforce that the change is still high on your agenda. Alternatively, you can introduce new goals into job descriptions that can be distinctly linked back to the change, further reinforcing that the new ways of operating are the *only* way to operate in your business.

4. Review how well your employees *fit* your business.
   Although the idea is less pleasant, a big change in a small business may mean that some individuals are no longer a good *fit*. Not all people may be able to make the change you require – it's not common, but it does happen. Individuals who cannot or will not change and have been given the opportunity to do so, may need to be offered alternatives inside or outside your business. Ultimately, it's OK for employees who don't or won't aspire to the Change Goal to move on.

5. Hire and promote with caution.
   When hiring new employees, make sure they are suitable for the new culture. Suitability of your employees means that their professional views and values align with the path you have taken your business on. Having the right expertise is important, but if they don't value the culture you're trying to build, you may be hiring a lot of new issues to deal with.

   Similarly, when promoting existing employees, make sure they are people who keenly adopted the change, that they believe in the future opportunities of the change, and willingly support others to create a better future for your business. Due to the public and visible nature of promotions, it's important that the person promoted symbolises the new ways of working.

WHAT TO DO NEXT

Managing change well is both hard work and rewarding in equal measure. Now is the time to reflect on how far your business has come and to acknowledge the collective effort to get there. The next exercise focuses on arranging a celebration to mark the end of your change-over period.

EXERCISE 14.3: CELEBRATE

The purpose of this exercise is to celebrate the achievement of the Change Goal and highlight the end of the project.

WHAT TO DO

1. Choose the type of celebration.

   Depending on the number of employees, business size, location and budget, you may choose to mark the achievement with a big celebration, or choose to do something small. Typically, the celebration should reflect the size of the contribution your employees made to the change effort.

2. Decide what to recognise. Then decide on who you want to recognise and why.

Recognition

Recognition is important for making employees feel appreciated and valued. Here are some examples:

- Efforts made by individuals who made a difference to the outcome
- Specific behaviour that demonstrated the new way of working
- Individuals or teams highly impacted by the change that showed resilience and acceptance
- Early adopters and role models or *experts*
- The extra effort put in by your Change Supporters
- Family and friends who supported key people, for example,

during weekend work or when travelling, or during other times of sacrifice.

3. Choose suitable gifts.

It's good form to distribute gifts or tokens of recognition during the celebration – wine, chocolates, gift certificates, that type of thing. You might do a speech and call on a range of people to share their experiences. Reflecting on the journey together is a good way to create a deeper bond with employees, appreciating the fact that together you *weathered the storm*.

4. Avoid these common mistakes when recognising people's efforts to adapt to change.

Avoid common mistakes

This advice may appear common sense but many business owners make these mistakes:

- Don't underestimate the power of celebration as a meaningful approach to reinforcing the change and maintaining employee engagement. Ignoring this step, or doing something on the cheap, may cause employees to resent that their efforts are not reflected fairly in the style of celebration – don't make this mistake. It is better to over-appreciate than to under-recognise because the next time you ask employees to pitch in, they'll remember what you did to reward their efforts on this occasion.
- Don't be insincere or trivialise the effort people have freely offered during the process.
- Don't use the occasion as a platform to introduce topics not associated with the change effort.
- Don't undermine your engagement effort by using this forum to point out weaknesses or failings – it's not the time or the place.

WHAT TO DO NEXT

Going out of your way to make people feel good about themselves will in turn encourage good feelings about your company and this helps the change to stick. After three months it's wise to check-in to ensure the change is still *sticking*. The next exercise focuses on determining how embedded the change is in business-as usual.

EXERCISE 14.4: GAUGING IF THE CHANGE IS STICKING

The purpose of this exercise is to look for indicators that the change has been adopted into your business.

WHAT TO DO

1. Look for leaders and supervisors freely supporting and reinforcing the change within their teams and encouraging those that fit in and disapproving of those who don't.

2. Look for employees actively role-modelling the change for new employees.

3. Listen to employees talking to customers about the change or creating new ways to get more from the benefits of the change without being prompted.

4. Look for decisions that reflect the Change Goal.

5. Look for instances where old behaviours and redundant work practices are used as examples to explain how your business has evolved.

6. Check that the performance and productivity benefits generated out of the change are being sustained.

7. Observe how your workforce continues to show signs of being engaged in the new working environment.

8. Ultimately you'll see it and feel it. Language and behaviour that demonstrates movement away from the change being *new* and becoming *the way we do things around here* is a good sign. For help identifying if employees are still not on board, refer below.

Demonstrations that employees aren't on board

Resistance is often obvious, but not always. Rejection of change can manifest in subtle ways. What's worse, it can be contagious. If it's not dealt with it can affect the mindsets of others.

Here are a few examples of warning signs that your employees might be resisting the change effort towards the end of the transition:

- Employees who are actively supporting the change are becoming frustrated.
- People who have resisted or appeared negative about the change in the past are getting more and more attention from other employees.
- Your Change Supporters are being criticised or employees are not seeking their advice or support on the change.
- The Change Goal is challenged, questioned or rubbished after the business has fully transitioned to the new mode of operation.
- Focus is directed to which of the old ways can be kept or maintained in the *new world*.
- Discussion is fixated on costs and sacrifices rather than future successes and opportunities.
- The majority of business decisions are still based on past successes and experiences.
- New recruits leave because they are frustrated in their efforts to fit in.

For help with dealing with resistance, refer to *Chapter 15 Dealing with Resistance.*

WHAT TO DO NEXT

Well done. You are at the end of the Transfer stage and have also completed the final stage of the Adapt Method. The next chapter focuses on how to deal with resistance before, during and after a change has taken place in your business.

SUMMARY

- Reinforce new behaviour in the ordinary day-to-day operations of your business.
- Reward employees who show others how the change looks when it's been adopted successfully.
- Collect and analyse data to monitor and track performance fluctuations, listen to feedback and encourage communication to gauge that the change has transferred into business-as-usual.
- Build the benefits of the new operating model into your future business objectives.
- Celebrate the efforts of your team; without them you couldn't have achieved your Change Goal.
- Deal with any subtle signs of resistance.

CHAPTER 15

DEALING WITH RESISTANCE

SUPREME EXCELLENCE CONSISTS IN BREAKING THE ENEMY'S RESISTANCE WITHOUT FIGHTING

SUN TZU - PHILOSOPHER

The greater the disruption caused by change, the higher the likelihood that employees will resist.

Resistance to change can quickly result in many undesirable consequences. Internally it can cause a reduction in customer service quality, produce an increase in absenteeism, and even result in good employees leaving. Externally it can lower loyalty and support for your brand, result in a loss of business or slowdown in growth, and cause damage to your reputation. Employee resistance is the biggest threat to the success of your Change Goal. The financial benefits of a change effort can be derailed if resistance is not dealt with in a timely and appropriate manner.

The purpose of this chapter is to equip you with practical strategies to deal with resistance in the workplace. Although it covers a wide range of resistant behaviours, not every incident you may encounter is covered; that would be impossible. But answers to address most typical human reactions in a changing environment can be found here.

In this chapter you will receive guidance on dealing with:
- employee resistance to change – refer to Table 15.1
- internal obstructions – refer to Table 15.2.

Using the information and tips in this chapter will help to diagnose what the cause of the resistance you're encountering is, and the ways to deal with it.

TABLE 15.1: TIPS FOR DEALING WITH EMPLOYEE RESISTANCE

To use this table, you need to:

1. Look down the *Resistant Behaviour* column and identify something that relates to your issue.

2. Check that the behaviour you have observed is similar to what is described in the *Possible Reasons* column.

3. If they align, use the recommendations in the *Tips* column to overcome the resistant behaviour.

Resistant Behaviour	Possible Reasons	Tips
Frustration	Employees may: • feel under-appreciated for the extra effort they've put into the change • think there's not enough time to learn or practise • think there's limited or no opportunity to participate • think they're not included in decisions that affect them • feel there is too much change, causing change fatigue.	• If frustration or scepticism is widespread – get feedback from across your business to understand the source of the problem. You could run an anonymous survey, or host group discussions. Perhaps a flaw in the logic has been identified. Or employees have lost faith in the goal. Whatever the cause, you need to find out to be able to get resistors back on track. • Agree to address the concern but seek commitment from resistors to contribute equally. That way there is effort on both sides. Act quickly. Employees lose trust and faith in leaders who take too long to make a decision or don't follow through. Then check-in with employees to make sure the problem has been resolved. • In addition, go back to basics. Re-communicate the Change Goal, the benefits, the reasons why the business must change and the risks of not changing.
Scepticism	Employees may: • challenge or question the benefits of the change or don't believe the change will benefit the business • not understand why the change is needed, or the consequences to the business of not changing • fear the change will have a negative impact on jobs, wages, incentives or bonuses • have the mindset of *We have always done it this way.*	

Resistant Behaviour	Possible Reasons	Tips
Reluctance to help	Employees may: • appear slow to get involved or make the change happen • avoid dealing with problems that arise during the change project • not understand the reasons why the business needs to change • believe their immediate supervisor is negative about the change or is creating barriers that are making it difficult for them to demonstrate the change.	• Don't present the process of implementing the change – new system, process, technology, etc. – as a done deal. Give employees an opportunity to participate in the planning and implementation. Ask them for ideas and feedback to show them their help is needed and valued. • Include employees in any decision that you make that affects them. It doesn't have to change the outcome, just let them know what's happening and allow them to voice their opinion about it. Open dialogue about change can diffuse the tension it creates. • Give resistors responsibilities. Allow them to lead an activity, or take an active role in something important in the change project. This demonstrates trust and inclusion. • If a resistor thinks they know a better way, allow them to test out their idea. If the idea is a success take it on board and give them credit – this is likely to diffuse their opposition and may even win them over to be a significant supporter of the change.

Complaining about lack of time	Employees may: • say they don't have enough time or complain of being tired • believe there are too many activities going on at once competing for their time and effort • think that the extra effort required to participate in the change is not being factored into their workflow • believe the change has increased their workload and the business is not being reasonable asking them to sustain it.	• Check that supervisors aren't being negative or discouraging employees to participate in change activities – gloomy comments from one individual can have an impact on everyone around them. • Always go back to basics. Re-communicate the Change Goal. What's in it for the employee must be crystal clear, as should the consequences to the business of not changing. • Review the workflow. If it has increased unreasonably, determine what tasks can be put on hold, redeployed to other team members, or are no longer required in the new operating model. Modify workflow across your business. Get feedback from employees to determine if this has relieved the pressure.

Resistant Behaviour	Possible Reasons	Tips
Complaining about lack of skill	Employees may: • lack confidence in their learning ability • feel they don't have the right skills to change their behaviour successfully • believe there is not enough on-the-job support, not enough training, or not enough time to learn new skills • be unclear about their role after it has been impacted by the change.	• The skills training may have been too superficial. You may need to introduce deeper learning sessions that cover a wider range of real-life scenarios. • Talk to the concerned employees to find out what support is being provided to them and why it isn't enough or the right kind of support. Change the support structure or introduce new elements to bolster their learning and practice. • Create on-the-job support tools for employees to refer to when they feel unsure of what to do. Be mindful that some employees need multiple opportunities to try out the new behaviours before they will really sink in. • Explain to leaders that new skills take time to adopt and perfect, that people learn at different rates, and empathy and understanding are needed to support people through change.
Making unreasonable mistakes	Employees may: • be afraid to try the new work practices because they believe that negative consequences exist in the environment and are applied when mistakes are made	• Expect leaders to offer support and encouragement. They should give recognition every time they see a small success. • Investigate what happens to employees when mistakes are made. If supervisors apply hostile corrective action, you need to fix this.

- view leaders or supervisors as being negative, lacking in empathy, creating roadblocks, or taking the attitude that employees should *just do it*
- feel there is not enough encouragement or support available for them to succeed
- lack the skill or knowledge needed to undertake the new work practices
- believe that a system or process is obstructing progress.

- Changes to roles must be clearly communicated. Check that supervisors have taken every team member through the impacts to their role. Ensure new tasks and responsibilities are documented, and a copy provided to the employee for reference.
- Encourage employees to ask questions or clarify the detail of their role changes. Multiple conversations may be needed to give employees time to adjust.
- Empower leaders to reward small achievements. Regularly encourage, motivate and ask for feedback while employees build their confidence in their decision-making abilities.
- Identify any managers who are being negative or not encouraging employees to practise. Coach them on their role as supporter of their team. Help them feel more in control and an important part of the change process. Get them on board; they need support and encouragement too.
- Find the system in your business that is stopping change from progressing. Repurpose that system to align with the new operating model or consider replacing it with a more suitable solution.

Resistant Behaviour	Possible Reasons	Tips
Unclear or confused about the impact on their role	Employees may: • be unclear about their duties after the change has taken place. Often the role doesn't align with the new system, process, task, etc. because the job description hasn't been changed.	• Communicate the new role descriptions with employees and highlight the changes that affect each person. • Provide coaching and on-the-job support tools like checklists, quick reference charts, how-to guides, etc. to support the completion of tasks.
Critical of the process for embedding the change into the business	Employees may: • not be clear on the scope and timeline for the change project, or the degree of impact to a team or individual • fear what's being sacrificed, lost, or given up in the change • see issues or inefficiencies in the change process.	• Re-communicate the Change Goal, what's in it for them and the consequences to the business of not changing. • Re-engage these employees with the new opportunities being gained from the change in direction or mode of operation. Ask what they need to feel comfortable with the change. Provide the extra support or reassurance they need. • Increase your communication effort by sending out targeted messages – the right message at the right time to the right people is the best approach. • Review the process you're using to introduce the change. Identify any flaws or blockages and remove them.

Saying 'I can't change'	Employees may: • appear adamant they can't or won't change • be unwilling to participate in change-related activities • be comfortable, or entrenched in the old ways of working • perceive there is no consequence to *not* complying with the change.	• Boost morale by introducing mechanisms to empower employees to maintain control over their environment during the transition. • In some cases people just can't adapt – they are limited by aptitude or willingness. Approach the person with empathy. Listen and respond with supportive ways to help the person overcome their reluctance to change. Take time to explain exactly what's in it for them – for example, opportunities to progress, to learn something new, to gain promotion, to earn more money and benefits etc.
Negative about the change	Employees may: • believe the new ways of operating don't work • fear that the change will have a negative impact on jobs, wages, workload, responsibilities, incentives or bonuses • feel they are losing something and not gaining anything • share their objections with others • lack awareness of the benefits of the change or the *what's in it for me?*	• Increase the support offered to these employees; assign a buddy, offer extra training, one-on-one coaching, etc. • Explain how remuneration and incentives will be handled in the future. Draw attention to how employees can perform well under the new operating model.

Resistant Behaviour	Possible Reasons	Tips
Negative about the change *(cont'd...)*	• lack influence over things that directly affect their work and around which they have talents, experience and expertise.	• Be transparent about job losses if that is a real consequence of the change. Highlight new opportunities for promotion or role creation now or in the future. Give a picture of how that employee can be part of those opportunities. Talk about what they need to do to be considered for promotion or for the new roles being created. Explain how that team member can be part of those opportunities. Listen and use empathy as the tool for dealing with fear-related issues. • Reaffirm that the change is happening and that it is their choice to jump on board. Be clear about what you will and won't tolerate from this point on. Present options, including redeployment to another role or options outside of your business. If the person chooses the latter, provide support, time and encouragement to find another job. • Consider appointing them as a Change Supporter. A responsible role in the change might convert their ability to be negative into a positive influence. If you can turn a strong resistor into a supporter you will cultivate an even stronger ally. • As a last resort, consider ceasing their employment or bring in outside help to address the problem.

| Leaders are not co-operating, or not allowing employees time to attend training or practise | Leaders may:
• be feeling that their position or power will be lost as a result of the change
• be feeling that the value of their personal knowledge and contribution will be reduced
• fear that they will look incompetent, or worse, the change is set up to cause *them* to fail
• believe there are competing priorities between the change effort and other significant business-as-usual activities
• feel disempowered to make decisions on priorities between the change activities and other tasks. | • The existence of politics, generational differences or tradition can impair adoption. Be tireless in checking in with your leaders and supervisors that they are positive and supportive about the change in their area. Apathy or negativity from a direct supervisor is highly de-motivating during a change.
• Track down unsupportive leaders, find out their views and engage them in conversation for the purpose of gently counteracting their assumptions and perceptions. Provide a good argument in favour of the change, help them to see and feel it the way you do. If there is a problem you can resolve, or additional support you can give, then do it. You need their help to make the change bear fruit.
• Make sure leaders develop rosters which are supportive and relieve employees to be able to attend training.
• Leaders need to help teams to reprioritise tasks to share the load while fellow team members are away from their work area. Be firm with supervisors that the learning activities are a priority. |

Resistant Behaviour	Possible Reasons	Tips
Leaders are not co-operating, or not allowing employees time to attend training or practise *(cont'd...)*		• Involve your leaders and supervisors in every stage of the change. Help them be part of the solution, not the problem. Make them see the change is happening *with* them, not *to* them. • Consider bringing in outside help to work with your leaders to break down the barriers they have created.
Disengaged	Employees may: • view the business leader as not being visible or not participating or role modelling the changed behaviours • believe their achievements are not being recognised and rewarded • feel they have limited or no ability to contribute to the change process • see a conflict between expectations and incentives when reward and recognition systems don't match the new work practices or business objectives.	• Be visible. Be out on the floor, in the workshop, the office, the garage, the shed, the warehouse – wherever your employees are. Be seen role-modelling the changed behaviour. You must demonstrate the behaviour you want your employees to adopt. • Reward small wins to demonstrate to your employees that their contribution is being noticed and is valued. Recognising small efforts is critical to demonstrating to your employees that something is happening – the change is having an effect. It provides tangible evidence that attempts to change

the business are paying off, that personal efforts to change are being rewarded, and that *the new way we do business around here* is valued.

- Involve employees in the change process. Are you allowing them to contribute to the design or shaping of the solution? This often results in positive word-of-mouth – just be sure you allow genuine input, not token, as this may have the reverse effect.

- Create feedback forums to give employees the opportunity to have a say about what's working and what's not, and how they're feeling about the change.

- Check that leaders and supervisors are not using a command-and-control management approach to leading their teams through the change. This can destabilise a whole change effort if left unchecked.

- Intensify engagement efforts. Bring in outside help to create a focused engagement strategy to address the specific problems.

Resistant Behaviour	Possible Reasons	Tips
No collaboration	Employees may: • perceive the communication about the change to be poor, insufficient or irrelevant, or given at the wrong time, or to the wrong audience • believe leaders and supervisors are protecting their *patch* and don't want to share or work together • be of the attitude that collaboration is not part of the business culture.	• Your Communications Plan and Engagement Plan are insufficient to support the change to your business. Go back and revise them. Give priority to activities that motivate employees to want to support the Change Goal. Make talking about the change and its business benefits part of every conversation and meeting in your business. • Identify teams that are operating in solo mode. Remind these employees that change is a team sport, not a solo pursuit. Ask questions like: What are you or your team doing to implement the change? What holds you back from collaborating? How can your team help other teams to make the change? • Get employees to create an action plan that focuses on collaborative activities. Support its implementation and reward employee efforts to collaborate, even the small gestures. Demonstrate you are serious about rewarding the right behaviours. Keep checking in to ensure teams don't become divisive again.

'If it ain't broke, don't fix it'	Employees may • view change as counter-cultural • hold the opinion *We've never needed to change before, so why now?*	• Communication is vital here. You need to spend time dealing with these mindsets. Approach with empathy. Openly discuss why they feel the way they do. Coach them on the benefits of moving to the new way of operating. • Strong attention needs to be put on the benefits for the future and consequences to the business if it doesn't change to meet market demands. • Your employees may be overly complacent or indifferent. Bringing in outside help to work with your team to break down this belief is useful for overcoming this problem.

Politicking, arguing, or anti-social behaviour or language has spiked	Employees may:
	• see the business as having a history of failing to implement change or as having introduced change badly in the past
	• be sceptical that other employees are willing to change
	• not believe the business can deliver the benefits of the change.
		• Past bad experiences cause people to think *here we go again*. Attack this problem head on. This type of negativism is like a virus and can infect your whole workforce.
		• There isn't a one-size-fits-all approach to this problem. Dealing with this will require effort and time from your employees and determination from you to stamp it out.
		• The principles recommended are:
		  · Listening
		  · Getting feedback
		  · Using empathy to draw out reasons for hostility

Resistant Behaviour	Possible Reasons	Tips
Politicking, arguing, or anti-social behaviour or language has spiked *(cont'd...)*		· Getting individuals to own the problem and the solution · Considering termination for serious offenders. • Bringing in outside help to deal with this problem may be vital to addressing it quickly.
Unexplained absenteeism	Employees may: • feel stressed • vulnerable • under too much pressure.	• Make sure your leaders understand the human reaction to change is fear, anxiety, loss of confidence, self-doubt – to name a few. Communication and engagement are vital ingredients to supporting employees through the change process. • Give leaders the authority to motivate using a method they believe will be effective and is tailored for their team. Use their close proximity and deeper relationship to address the problem. • Re-evaluate people's workload, ease off pressure, re-define priorities and expectations. • Be more visible to employees and interact with them daily to demonstrate that you hear them and they have your support.

Reverting back to old ways	Employees may: • adopt the change initially but then give up and revert back to their old way of working.	• Communication and engagement activities that are stopped too early after the change is embedded in the business are often the reason for this problem. Go back to your Communications Plan and Engagement Plan and build in more activities that motivate employees to believe in, and want to support, the Change Goal. • Trace the cause. Is there a fault in the process, or a flaw in the data, or a bug in the system, or a lack of skill? If it's data, process or system based, rectify the problem. If it's skill based, provide one-on-one coaching to re-train employees in the right way to perform the task. • Bringing in outside help to work with your team to address this scenario is useful to overcome the problem.

TABLE 15.2: TIPS FOR DEALING WITH OBSTRUCTIONS CREATED BY INTERNAL SYSTEMS

To use this table, you need to:

1. Look down the *Indicator* column and identify something that relates to your issue.

2. Check that your observation is similar to what is described in the *Possible Cause* column.

3. If they align, then use the recommendations in the *Tips* column to overcome obstructions in your internal operating systems.

Indicator	Possible Cause	Tips
Performance has declined	There are numerous potential causes for this problem. For example: • time spent on the change effort is causing too much of a distraction to business-as-usual activity. • employees are taken away from their work to attend training and coaching sessions without someone being available to backfill them.	• This problem is not always a result of resistance, although it can often be assumed to be. It is common during an intensive period of change for business-as-usual performance levels to decline somewhat. Employees are using a lot of energy, effort and headspace to make the change work. This is a normal consequence of people trying to change and spending time learning new skills. • However, should you see a deeper downward trend, then performance indicators need to be analysed to identify the source. Once the problem has been found, empower your team to formulate a solution and get them to introduce it.
The change is being implemented too slowly	• The impact to employees was underestimated and not remedied. • Leaders are creating obstacles. • Insufficient time or resource has been dedicated to the change effort. • Goal posts are shifting – priorities, objectives, or the Change Goal moves without replanning.	• Go back to basics. Check which tasks need to be performed differently, or will no longer exist against your original impact assessment. What has been overlooked? What time span was predicted to make the change? What time is still needed? Are there obstacles to employees being able to change? Modify the approach being used. Keep altering the approach until the pace of change is satisfactory.

Indicator	Possible Cause	Tips
The change is being implemented too slowly *(cont'd...)*		• If the problem is widespread find out why. Understand the cause. Where are employees spending too much time or effort? Is it required? Is there a better way of achieving the same outcome? • Check that leaders are giving priority to the change activities. Provide guidance and support to leaders who need to adopt a more collaborative approach with their teams. • Seek outside advice on the progress of the change – is it realistic to expect implementation to happen in the timeframe you have set? Investigate what part of the change effort is taking too long. Identify the reason for the time lag. Are employees clear on what they need to do? Do they have the right skills? Do they have the right support or resources?
Overtime has unreasonably increased	• Employees are working long hours to make the change work because the impact to them has been underestimated.	• If you alter the Change Goal you will need to replan your change activities to support the new direction.

- If the Change Goal is the same, identify what might be causing the need for overtime by talking to your team. Are you expecting change to happen too quickly? Is your planning detailed enough to fully support your business during this time? What will remedy the problem? Ask employees for their ideas on how to streamline activities, what can be left out, or done at a later time. What's critical, and what's not? Agree a suitable work schedule and ask employees to stick to it. Review the situation regularly.
- Employees who are tired or burnt out are not going to perform well. Have realistic expectations. You may need to rethink what can be achieved in the allotted timeframe.

| **Incompatibility between new and old** | • Internal systems continue to support or encourage the old way of working. | • If the new operating model is incompatible with existing systems, chances are that people's behaviour will be slow to change or will revert back to the old ways. For example, appraisal, incentive and promotion systems need to be in harmony with the *new ways* for the change to succeed.
• Find the incompatibility and remedy it. |

SUMMARY

- Resistance to change is a normal part of the human condition.
- Resistance can arise at any time throughout a change effort and if it's not dealt with properly, it can affect other employees or spread to other sections of your business.
- Ways of dealing with resistance centre on communication, engagement and empathy.

CHAPTER 16
WHERE TO FROM HERE

Thank you for taking the time to read *Adopt Adapt Flourish*. If you have reached this page and done everything in the *Adapt Method*, I am absolutely certain that you will have introduced change to grow your business in a way that is rich and rewarding.

The reason I came to write this book was because the change management industry has, for the most part, been targeting large corporate organisations. Many change management tools and techniques are difficult to implement in a small business context; they take too long, need too much manpower, and suggest activities that aren't relevant to managing change in a small to medium enterprise. Yet there is so much value to be gained by small business from the change management discipline. Unlike big corporations whose wheels turn ever so slowly, small business has a much greater need to be agile and flex with the adjustments in the economy and global markets. The guidance I have provided is just the beginning of what is possible to foster a highly engaged workforce and manage people through change effectively.

My aim for this book was to empower everyday business owners to thrive as they grow their business and to get the most out of their workforce with the least resistance and stress, in the least amount of time. I hope your business is one of them.

If you want to experience more ways to successfully engage your employees, please visit *www.adaptusconsulting.com.au*. If this book has inspired you, I would love to hear your story. Please contact me at melanie@adaptusconsulting.com.au

RECOMMENDED READING

I am often asked about books that influenced me as I developed my consulting career. These are listed below. The philosophies and principles of these world-renowned authors underpin the methods in this book. If you want to learn more about how to manage change in your business, I recommend reading the following books.

Getting to the Heart of Employee Engagement – The Power and Purpose of Imagination and Free Will in the Workplace, Les Landes, ISBN 9781475947991

Leading Change, John P Kotter, ISBN 139781422186435

Fish! Omnibus – A Remarkable Way to Boost Morale and Improve Results, Stephen C Lundin, PhD, Harry Paul, and John Christensen, ISBN 9780340924587

ADKAR: A Model for Change in Business, Government and our Community, Jeffrey M Hiatt, ISBN 1930885504

CHAPTER 16

Beyond Performance – How Great Organizations Build Ultimate Competitive Advantage, Scott Keller and Colin Price, ISBN 9781118024621

ABOUT THE AUTHOR

Melanie Frok is the founder of Adaptus Consulting, a business offering tailored coaching and strategic solutions to business owners who want to build their business's change management and employee engagement capability.

Melanie's methods take the hassle out of introducing something new by ensuring everything goes smoothly while you run your business. She is someone who is truly qualified to call herself a Business Change Expert.

Melanie is passionate about using employee engagement as the platform to grow a business and see it flourish. She devotes her time to working with leading businesses to find unique and effective ways to ensure their employees adapt to change faster, are fully engaged, and able to perform effectively. Over the past twenty years, Melanie has helped people embrace change in small, medium and corporate environments within the finance, banking, digital, commercial and local government sectors in Australia, Asia and the UK. Melanie's background and her unique business experience make her a rare talent in the business coaching industry.

For tailored advice, coaching, employee engagement and change management solutions, please contact Melanie at:

www.adaptusconsulting.com.au
melanie@adaptusconsulting.com.au